PSSA Math workbook

7th Grade Math Exercises, Activities, and Two Full-Length PSSA Math Practice Tests

By

Michael Smith & Reza Nazari

PSSA Math Workbook

Published in the United State of America By

The Math Notion

Email: info@Mathnotion.com

Web: www.MathNotion.com

About the Author

Michael Smith has been a math instructor for over a decade now. He holds a master's degree in Management. Since 2006, Michael has devoted his time to both teaching and developing exceptional math learning materials. As a Math instructor and test prep expert, Michael has worked with thousands of students. He has used the feedback of his students to develop a unique study program that can be used by students to drastically improve their math score fast and effectively.

- **SAT Math Workbook**
- **PSAT Math Workbook**
- **ACT Math Workbook**
- **GRE Math Workbook**
- **Common Core Math Workbook**
- **many Math Education Workbooks**
- **and some Mathematics books ...**

As an experienced Math teacher, Mr. Smith employs a variety of formats to help students achieve their goals: He tutors online and in person, he teaches students in large groups, and he provides training materials and textbooks through his website and through Amazon.

You can contact Michael via email at:
info@Mathnotion.com

PSSA Math Workbook

PSSA Math Workbook reviews all PSSA Math topics and provides students with the confidence and math skills they need to succeed on the PSSA Math. It is designed to address the needs of PSSA test takers who must have a working knowledge of basic Mathematics.

This comprehensive workbook with over 2,500 sample questions and 2 complete PSSA tests can help you fully prepare for the PSSA Math test. It provides you with an in-depth focus on the math portion of the exam, helping you master the math skills that students find the most troublesome. This is an incredibly useful tool for those who want to review all topics being covered on the PSSA Math test.

PSSA Math Workbook contains many exciting features to help you prepare for the PSSA Math test, including:

- Content 100% aligned with the 2019-2020 PSSA test
- Provided and tested by PSSA Math test experts
- Dynamic design and easy-to-follow activities
- A fun, interactive and concrete learning process
- Targeted, skill-building practices
- Complete coverage of all PSSA Math topics which you will be tested
- 2 full-length practice tests (featuring new question types) with detailed answers.

The only prep book you will ever need to ace the PSSA Math Test!

WWW.MathNotion.COM

… So Much More Online!

✓ FREE Math Lessons

✓ More Math Learning Books!

✓ Mathematics Worksheets

✓ Online Math Tutors

For a PDF Version of This Book

Please Visit WWW.MathNotion.com

Contents

Chapter 1: Real Numbers and Integers

Topics that you'll learn in this chapter:

- ✓ Adding and Subtracting Integers

- ✓ Multiplying and Dividing Integers

- ✓ Ordering Integers and Numbers

- ✓ Arrange, Order, and Comparing Integers

- ✓ Order of Operations

- ✓ Mixed Integer Computations

- ✓ Absolute Value

- ✓ Integers and Absolute Value

- ✓ Classifying Real Numbers Venn Diagram

Adding and Subtracting Integers

✐Find the sum.

1) (– 17) + (– 3)

2) 15 + (– 25)

3) (– 15) + 35

4) (– 10) + (32)

5) 55 + (–24)

6) (– 28) + (– 16) + 13

7) 18 + (– 26) + (– 15) + (– 45)

8) 20 + (– 13) + 17 + 11

9) (– 18) + (– 24) + (25 – 13)

10) 13 + (– 27) + (39 – 26)

✐Find the difference.

11) (– 13) – (– 18) – (6)

12) (– 18) – (– 25)

13) (– 24) – (17)

14) (36) – (– 14)

15) (53) – (12)

16) (26) – (– 16) + (– 8)

17) (20) – (8) – (– 15)

18) (12) – (6) – (– 3)

19) (24) – (6) – (– 44)

20) (– 58) – (– 75)

Multiplying and Dividing Integers

✏️ **Find each product.**

1) $(-4) \times (-3)$

2) 6×5

3) $(-4) \times 2 \times (-8)$

4) $9 \times (-2) \times (-5)$

5) $12 \times (-11)$

6) $10 \times (-5)$

7) 8×8

8) $(-5) \times (-9)$

9) $4 \times (-7) \times 5$

10) $8 \times (-1) \times 4$

✏️ **Find each quotient.**

11) $16 \div 2$

12) $(-81) \div 3$

13) $(-56) \div (-7)$

14) $56 \div 8$

15) $80 \div (-4)$

16) $(-77) \div (-11)$

17) $121 \div 11$

18) $(-169) \div 13$

19) $88 \div 4$

20) $36 \div 6$

Ordering Integers and Numbers

✍ Order each set of integers from least to greatest.

1) $-19, -15, 20, -3, 1$ ___, ___, ___, ___, ___, ___

2) $16, -17, 11, -8, 14$ ___, ___, ___, ___, ___, ___

3) $-15, -48, 19, 0, -26, 5$ ___, ___, ___, ___, ___, ___

4) $106, -56, 0, -28, 86, -66$ ___, ___, ___, ___, ___, ___

5) $-19, -18, 30, -25, -24, -39$ ___, ___, ___, ___, ___, ___

6) $89, 55, 64, 19, 7, 2$ ___, ___, ___, ___, ___, ___

✍ Order each set of integers from greatest to least.

7) $3, -4, 2, -7, -5$ ___, ___, ___, ___, ___, ___

8) $-38, 18, -18, -25, 12$ ___, ___, ___, ___, ___, ___

9) $22, -37, -18, -17, 14$ ___, ___, ___, ___, ___, ___

10) $74, 62, 55, -18, 96, 82$ ___, ___, ___, ___, ___, ___

11) $-5, -7, -12, -4, -6, -21$ ___, ___, ___, ___, ___, ___

12) $-28, -31, -25, -23, 0, 2$ ___, ___, ___, ___, ___, ___

Arrange, Order, and Comparing Integers

✍ **Arrange these integers in descending order.**

1) $44, 18, -18, -22, 99$ ___, ___, ___, ___, ___, ___

2) $14, 17, 42, -12, -8, -5$ ___, ___, ___, ___, ___, ___

3) $-15, 36, 17, 15, -17$ ___, ___, ___, ___, ___, ___

4) $-12, -17, 4, 9, -13$ ___, ___, ___, ___, ___, ___

5) $36, -36, -16, -18, -46$ ___, ___, ___, ___, ___, ___

✍ *Compare. Use* >, =, <

6) -9 ___ -13

7) -11 ___ 17

8) 98 ___ 89

9) 17 ___ $-(-17)$

10) -365 ___ -355

11) -65 ___ -68

12) 55 ___ 36

13) -99 ___ -101

14) -1006 ___ -1006

15) -623 ___ -723

Order of Operations

✍ **Evaluate each expression.**

1) $(4 \times 3) + 2$

2) $36 - (4 \times 4)$

3) $(8 \times 2) + 15$

4) $24 - (7 \times 3)$

5) $(6 \times 5) + 5$

6) $91 - (9 \times 9)$

7) $27 + (2 \times 9)$

8) $(7 \times 7) + 9$

9) $60 \div (16 + 4)$

10) $(16 + 12) \div (- 7)$

11) $17 + (5 \times 2) - 6$

12) $(6 + 4) \times \frac{4}{5} + 1$

13) $3 \times 8 - (\frac{18}{9 - 3})$

14) $(15 + 12 - 16) \times 5 - 20$

15) $(\frac{9}{8 - 3}) \times (1 + 4) \times 3$

16) $49 \div (10 - (12 - 9))$

17) $\frac{35}{5\,(8 - 6) - 5}$

18) $14 + (4 \times 12)$

Mixed Integer Computations

✍ **Compute.**

1) $(- 80) \div (- 8)$

2) $(- 24) \times 2$

3) $(- 7) \times (- 15)$

4) $(- 75) \div 15$

5) $17 \times (- 7)$

6) $(- 7) \times (- 4)$

7) $\frac{(- 40)}{(- 20)}$

8) $48 \div (- 8)$

9) $55 \div (- 11)$

10) $\frac{(- 40)}{8}$

11) $5 \times (-6)$

12) $\frac{(-98)}{14}$

13) $(-13) \times (-3)$

14) $(-8) \times (-7)$

15) $\frac{-36}{-6}$

16) $(-66) \div 11$

17) $(-80) \div (-2)$

18) $(-8) \times (-19)$

19) $(-17) \times 20$

20) $81 \div (-9)$

Absolute Value

✎Evaluate.

1) $|-4| + |-11| - 8$

2) $|-16| + |-4|$

3) $-13 + |-8+5| - 11$

4) $|16| \div |4|$

5) $|-7| \div |-1|$

6) $|900| \div |-10|$

7) $|77| \div |11|$

8) $|81| \div |-9|$

9) $|4| \times |-6|$

10) $|-30| \times |-7|$

11) $|16| \times |-2|$

12) $|15| \times |-7|$

13) $|-17| \times |3|$

14) $|-9| \times |-5|$

15) $|52-65+18| + |-23| - 12$

16) $|-53+85| + |36| - |24|$

17) $90 + |-19-25| - |24|$

18) $|-15+26| + |20+4| - 10$

Integers and Absolute Value

✎ Write absolute value of each number.

1) – 6
2) – 18
3) – 100
4) 16
5) – 17
6) – 14
7) 20

8) – 15
9) 34
10) – 35
11) – 13
12) 16
13) – 30
14) 19

15) – 47
16) – 29
17) – 100
18) – 61
19) 110
20) – 76
21) – 800

✎ Evaluate.

22) $|-30| - |20| + 22$

23) $75 + |-36 - 45| - |20|$

24) $55 + |-46| - 90$

25) $|86| - |-42| + 92$

26) $|-42 + 3| + 6 - 1$

27) $|-13| + |-13|$

28) $|-15 + 12 - 24| + |12 + 21|$

29) $|-28| + |-45| - 45$

Classifying Real Numbers Venn Diagram

✎ Identify all the subsets of real number system to which each number belongs.

1) 10
2) – 8
3) – 11.25
4) $\sqrt{36}$

5) 12
6) 1000
7) – 8
8) $2 \times \pi$

9) $\frac{2}{5}$
10) $\frac{10}{2}$
11) $\sqrt{11}$

Answers of Worksheets – Chapter 1

Adding and Subtracting Integers

1) – 20
2) – 10
3) 20
4) 22
5) 31
6) – 31
7) –68
8) 35
9) – 30
10) – 1
11) –1
12) 7
13) – 41
14) 50
15) 41
16) 34
17) 27
18) 9
19) 62
20) 17

Multiplying and Dividing Integers

1) 12
2) 30
3) 64
4) 90
5) – 132
6) – 50
7) 64
8) 45
9) – 140
10) – 32
11) 8
12) – 27
13) 8
14) 7
15) -20
16) 7
17) 11
18) -13
19) 22
20) 6

Ordering Integers and Numbers

1) – 19, – 15, – 3, 1, 20
2) – 17, – 8 , 11, 14, 16
3) – 48, – 26, −15, 0, 5, 19
4) – 66, – 56, – 28, 0, 86, 106
5) – 39, – 25, – 24, – 19, – 18, 30
6) 2, 7, 19, 55, 64, 89
7) 3, 2, – 4, – 5, – 7
8) 18, 12, −18, −25, – 38
9) −37, −18, −17, 14, 22
10) 96, 82, 74, 62, 55, – 18
11) −4, −5, −6, −7, −12, −21
12) 2, 0, −23, −25, −28, −31

Arrange and Order, Comparing Integers

1) 99, 44, 18, – 18, – 22
2) 42, 17, 14, – 5, – 8, – 12
3) 36, 17, 15, – 15, –17
4) 9, 4, –12, –13, – 17
5) 36, –16, – 18, – 36, – 46

6) >
7) <
8) >
9) =
10) <
11) >
12) >
13) >
14) =
15) >

Order of Operations

1) 14
2) 20
3) 31
4) 3
5) 35
6) 10
7) 45
8) 58
9) 3

10) – 4
11) 21
12) 9

13) 21
14) 35
15) 27

16) 7
17) 7
18) 62

Mixed Integer Computations

1) 10
2) – 48
3) 105
4) –5
5) – 119

6) 28
7) 2
8) – 6
9) – 5
10) – 5

11) – 30
12) – 7
13) 39
14) 56
15) 6

16) -6
17) 40
18) 152
19) – 340
20) – 9

Absolute Value

1) 7
2) 20
3) – 21
4) 4
5) 7
6) 90

7) 7
8) 9
9) 24
10) 210
11) 32
12) 105

13) 51
14) 45
15) 16
16) 44
17) 110
18) 25

Integers and Absolute Value

1) 6
2) 18
3) 100
4) 16
5) 17
6) 14
7) 20
8) 15
9) 34
10) 35

11) 13
12) 16
13) 30
14) 19
15) 47
16) 29
17) 100
18) 61
19) 110
20) 76

21) 800
22) 32
23) 136
24) 11
25) 136
26) 44
27) 26
28) 60
29) 28

Classifying Real Numbers Venn Diagram

1) 10: whole number, integer, rational number

2) – 8: integer, rational number

3) – 11.25: rational number

4) $\sqrt{36}$: natural number, whole number, integer, rational number

5) 12: natural number, whole number, integer, rational number

6) 1000: natural number, whole number, integer, rational number

7) -8: whole number, integer, rational number

8) $2 \times \pi$: irrational number

9) $\frac{2}{5}$: rational number

10) $\frac{10}{2}$: natural number, integer, rational number

11) $\sqrt{11}$: irrational number

Chapter 2: Fractions and Decimals

Topics that you'll learn in this chapter:

- ✓ Factoring Numbers
- ✓ Greatest Common Factor
- ✓ Least Common Multiple
- ✓ Divisibility Rules
- ✓ Simplifying Fractions
- ✓ Adding and Subtracting Fractions
- ✓ Multiplying and Dividing Fractions
- ✓ Adding and Subtract Mixed Numbers
- ✓ Multiplying and Dividing Mixed Numbers
- ✓ Comparing Decimals
- ✓ Rounding Decimals
- ✓ Adding and Subtracting Decimals
- ✓ Multiplying and Dividing Decimals
- ✓ Converting Between Fractions, Decimals and Mixed Numbers

Factoring Numbers

✍ **List all positive factors of each number.**

1) 54	6) 99	11) 62
2) 80	7) 76	12) 75
3) 58	8) 14	13) 33
4) 39	9) 52	14) 60
5) 72	10) 43	15) 17

✍ **List the prime factorization for each number.**

16) 20	21) 48	26) 40
17) 45	22) 64	27) 12
18) 51	23) 22	28) 63
19) 95	24) 88	29) 18
20) 32	25) 16	30) 34

Greatest Common Factor

✏️ **Find the GCF for each number pair.**

1) 20, 30

2) 14, 12

3) 5, 35

4) 43, 7

5) 25, 15

6) 15, 45

7) 6, 24

8) 21, 14

9) 8, 16

10) 11, 3

11) 10, 45

12) 6, 48

13) 6, 24

14) 90, 10

15) 18, 36

16) 80, 25

17) 14, 77

18) 16, 14

19) 100, 25

20) 77, 35

21) 15, 50

22) 48, 42

23) 12, 72

24) 16, 8

Least Common Multiple

✎ **Find the LCM for each number pair.**

1) 4, 16

2) 3, 19

3) 6, 14

4) 4, 24

5) 8, 3

6) 8, 45

7) 15, 10

8) 9, 7

9) 19, 17

10) 12, 72

11) 5, 11

12) 13, 9

13) 2, 12

14) 12, 48

15) 60, 10, 20

16) 35, 5, 6

17) 32, 6, 16

18) 18, 12, 10

19) 7, 3, 12

20) 24, 4, 2

21) 6, 42

22) 82, 72

23) 36, 9

24) 24, 26, 15

Divisibility Rules

✍ **Use the divisibility rules to find the factors of each number.**

1) 14   2   3   4   5   6   7   8   9   10

2) 80   2   3   4   5   6   7   8   9   10

3) 28   2   3   4   5   6   7   8   9   10

4) 30   2   3   4   5   6   7   8   9   10

5) 44   2   3   4   5   6   7   8   9   10

6) 52   2   3   4   5   6   7   8   9   10

7) 25   2   3   4   5   6   7   8   9   10

8) 75   2   3   4   5   6   7   8   9   10

9) 36   2   3   4   5   6   7   8   9   10

10) 48   2   3   4   5   6   7   8   9   10

11) 72   2   3   4   5   6   7   8   9   10

12) 180   2   3   4   5   6   7   8   9   10

Simplifying Fractions

✍**Simplify the fractions.**

1) $\dfrac{8}{16}$

2) $\dfrac{9}{18}$

3) $\dfrac{5}{20}$

4) $\dfrac{15}{10}$

5) $\dfrac{9}{54}$

6) $\dfrac{11}{77}$

7) $\dfrac{6}{24}$

8) $\dfrac{9}{15}$

9) $\dfrac{30}{90}$

10) $\dfrac{3}{24}$

11) $\dfrac{14}{54}$

12) $\dfrac{22}{33}$

13) $\dfrac{15}{27}$

14) $\dfrac{23}{46}$

15) $\dfrac{12}{36}$

16) $\dfrac{18}{48}$

17) $\dfrac{16}{36}$

18) $\dfrac{40}{80}$

19) $\dfrac{3}{21}$

20) $\dfrac{10}{100}$

21) $\dfrac{25}{50}$

22) $\dfrac{32}{24}$

23) $\dfrac{15}{45}$

24) $\dfrac{121}{132}$

Adding and Subtracting Fractions

✎ Add fractions.

1) $\dfrac{3}{7}+\dfrac{1}{3}$

2) $\dfrac{4}{3}+\dfrac{2}{5}$

3) $\dfrac{1}{8}+\dfrac{3}{4}$

4) $\dfrac{1}{4}+\dfrac{2}{3}$

5) $\dfrac{1}{6}+\dfrac{5}{6}$

6) $\dfrac{5}{6}+\dfrac{1}{7}$

7) $\dfrac{5}{4}+\dfrac{3}{5}$

8) $\dfrac{3}{7}+\dfrac{2}{5}$

9) $\dfrac{2}{3}+\dfrac{4}{7}$

10) $\dfrac{4}{3}+\dfrac{7}{3}$

✎ Subtract fractions.

11) $\dfrac{3}{4}-\dfrac{1}{3}$

12) $\dfrac{1}{2}-\dfrac{3}{8}$

13) $\dfrac{1}{2}-\dfrac{2}{5}$

14) $\dfrac{7}{8}-\dfrac{1}{4}$

15) $\dfrac{3}{4}-\dfrac{1}{12}$

16) $\dfrac{2}{7}-\dfrac{1}{21}$

17) $\dfrac{11}{18}-\dfrac{1}{9}$

18) $\dfrac{7}{9}-\dfrac{1}{3}$

Multiplying and Dividing Fractions

✎ **Multiplying fractions. Then simplify.**

1) $\dfrac{1}{3} \times \dfrac{5}{7}$

2) $\dfrac{2}{7} \times \dfrac{3}{5}$

3) $\dfrac{5}{4} \times \dfrac{3}{7}$

4) $\dfrac{2}{7} \times \dfrac{3}{2}$

5) $\dfrac{1}{4} \times \dfrac{5}{11}$

6) $\dfrac{2}{5} \times \dfrac{1}{9}$

7) $\dfrac{3}{4} \times \dfrac{7}{5}$

8) $\dfrac{1}{3} \times \dfrac{1}{2}$

9) $\dfrac{3}{5} \times \dfrac{5}{8}$

10) $\dfrac{7}{12} \times \dfrac{4}{3}$

✎ **Dividing fractions.**

11) $\dfrac{5}{7} \div \dfrac{1}{14}$

12) $\dfrac{1}{3} \div \dfrac{4}{3}$

13) $\dfrac{3}{8} \div \dfrac{1}{4}$

14) $\dfrac{11}{14} \div \dfrac{2}{7}$

15) $\dfrac{5}{6} \div \dfrac{7}{12}$

16) $\dfrac{1}{8} \div \dfrac{3}{8}$

17) $\dfrac{4}{9} \div \dfrac{1}{9}$

18) $\dfrac{11}{15} \div \dfrac{11}{30}$

19) $\dfrac{5}{12} \div \dfrac{15}{24}$

Adding Mixed Numbers

✎ Add.

1) $6\frac{1}{2} + 4\frac{1}{2}$

2) $3\frac{1}{3} + 5\frac{2}{3}$

3) $6\frac{1}{6} + 3\frac{1}{6}$

4) $4\frac{1}{4} + 2\frac{3}{4}$

5) $3\frac{1}{7} + 2\frac{2}{7}$

6) $8\frac{1}{3} + 2\frac{2}{3}$

7) $4\frac{7}{11} + 2\frac{3}{11}$

8) $2\frac{1}{5} + 1\frac{4}{5}$

9) $3\frac{2}{7} + 2\frac{4}{7}$

10) $8 + \frac{1}{3}$

11) $3\frac{2}{5} + \frac{4}{5}$

12) $4\frac{1}{3} + 2\frac{1}{2}$

Subtract Mixed Numbers

✎ Subtract.

1) $4\frac{1}{3} - 2\frac{1}{3}$

2) $3\frac{4}{7} - 2\frac{3}{7}$

3) $7\frac{2}{9} - 3\frac{1}{9}$

4) $2\frac{5}{8} - 1\frac{1}{8}$

5) $6\frac{1}{4} - 3\frac{3}{4}$

6) $4\frac{2}{5} - 1\frac{1}{5}$

7) $3\frac{7}{9} - 2\frac{2}{3}$

8) $5\frac{1}{6} - 4\frac{1}{6}$

9) $5\frac{2}{7} - 3\frac{1}{7}$

10) $7\frac{4}{5} - 3\frac{1}{5}$

11) $3\frac{4}{9} - 1\frac{1}{9}$

12) $7\frac{1}{2} - 6\frac{1}{2}$

Multiplying Mixed Numbers

✏️ **Find each product.**

1) $2\frac{1}{3} \times 1\frac{1}{3}$

2) $4\frac{2}{5} \times 1\frac{1}{5}$

3) $1\frac{1}{4} \times 4\frac{2}{3}$

4) $3\frac{1}{5} \times 2\frac{2}{3}$

5) $4\frac{3}{4} \times 2\frac{1}{3}$

6) $2\frac{1}{3} \times 1\frac{1}{2}$

7) $2\frac{3}{8} \times 2\frac{1}{2}$

8) $3\frac{2}{5} \times 2\frac{1}{5}$

9) $3\frac{1}{2} \times 5\frac{1}{7}$

10) $7\frac{3}{5} \times 1\frac{1}{3}$

11) $4\frac{1}{3} \times 1\frac{1}{4}$

12) $3\frac{2}{5} \times 1\frac{2}{3}$

Dividing Mixed Numbers

✎ Find each quotient

1) $1\frac{1}{4} \div 1\frac{1}{2}$

2) $3\frac{2}{5} \div 1\frac{1}{2}$

3) $4\frac{2}{5} \div 1\frac{2}{7}$

4) $3\frac{2}{5} \div 1\frac{2}{3}$

5) $3\frac{1}{8} \div 2\frac{1}{4}$

6) $5\frac{1}{3} \div 2\frac{1}{2}$

7) $4\frac{1}{9} \div 1\frac{3}{5}$

8) $3\frac{3}{5} \div 4\frac{1}{5}$

9) $3\frac{1}{6} \div 2\frac{2}{5}$

10) $4\frac{3}{7} \div 2\frac{7}{6}$

11) $3\frac{1}{4} \div 1\frac{2}{5}$

12) $4\frac{2}{3} \div 2\frac{1}{3}$

13) $2\frac{1}{4} \div 2\frac{5}{7}$

14) $4\frac{7}{8} \div 4\frac{1}{5}$

15) $2\frac{2}{5} \div 3\frac{1}{6}$

16) $7\frac{2}{5} \div 2\frac{1}{5}$

Comparing Decimals

✍ **Write the correct comparison symbol (>, < or =).**

1) 2.26 _ 2.29

2) 1.5 _ 0.75

3) 5.1 _ 5.1

4) 6.48 _ 64.8

5) 3.95 _ 0.395

6) 8.2 _ 8

7) 9.1 _ 0.96

8) 4.13 _ 0.813

9) 10 _ 0.99

10) 6.65 _ 0.995

11) 2.43 _ 2.45

12) 6.66 _ 6.67

13) 8.08 _ 8.12

14) 1.11 _ 0.111

15) 5.8 _ 5.76

16) 3.32 _ 3.37

17) 8.32 _ 0.832

18) 0.13 _ 0.013

19) 63.7 _ 63.7

20) 0.03 _ 0.30

21) 0.59 _ 0.6

22) 0.7 _ 0.07

23) 0.80 _ 0.8

24) 0.46 _ 0.54

Rounding Decimals

✍ **Round each decimal number to the nearest place indicated.**

1) 0.2̲4

2) 3.0̲3

3) 6.6̲12

4) 0.2̲98

5) 6̲.32

6) 0.8̲6

7) 8.2̲1

8) 7̲.0432

9) 1.92̲6

10)   7.3̲654

11)   1̲.9

12)   5̲.1239

13)   6.8̲67

14)   8.5̲1

15)   90̲.84

16)   85̲.68

17)   75.7̲7

18)   635̲.611

19)   16̲.1

20)   85̲.98

21)   2̲.147

22)   86̲.4

23)   116.5̲13

24)   8.0̲7

Adding and Subtracting Decimals

✍ **Add and subtract decimals.**

1)
$$\begin{array}{r} 12.54 \\ -\ 11.56 \\ \hline \end{array}$$

4)
$$\begin{array}{r} 34.56 \\ -\ 23.83 \\ \hline \end{array}$$

2)
$$\begin{array}{r} 84.96 \\ +\ 34.67 \\ \hline \end{array}$$

5)
$$\begin{array}{r} 48.39 \\ +\ 68.95 \\ \hline \end{array}$$

3)
$$\begin{array}{r} 44.53 \\ +\ 33.28 \\ \hline \end{array}$$

6)
$$\begin{array}{r} 41.23 \\ -\ 19.84 \\ \hline \end{array}$$

✍ **Solve.**

7) ____ $+ 1.8 = 6.4$

11) ____ $+ 2.2 = 7.5$

8) $4.1 +$ ____ $= 13.4$

12) ____ $+ 7.8 = 17.8$

9) $7.9 +$ ____ $= 15$

13) ____ $+ 3.2 = 15.8$

10) $3.8 +$ ____ $= 15.9$

14) ____ $+ 0.8 = 10.8$

Multiplying and Dividing Decimals

✍ **Find each product.**

1)
$$\begin{array}{r} 1.2 \\ \times\ 2.4 \\ \hline \end{array}$$

4)
$$\begin{array}{r} 4.2 \\ \times\ 6.3 \\ \hline \end{array}$$

7)
$$\begin{array}{r} 3.5 \\ \times\ 2.2 \\ \hline \end{array}$$

2)
$$\begin{array}{r} 4.5 \\ \times\ 2.2 \\ \hline \end{array}$$

5)
$$\begin{array}{r} 11.2 \\ \times\ 12.6 \\ \hline \end{array}$$

8)
$$\begin{array}{r} 97.15 \\ \times\ 100 \\ \hline \end{array}$$

3)
$$\begin{array}{r} 2.6 \\ \times\ 1.4 \\ \hline \end{array}$$

6)
$$\begin{array}{r} 3.8 \\ \times\ 2.1 \\ \hline \end{array}$$

9)
$$\begin{array}{r} 29.98 \\ \times\ 1000 \\ \hline \end{array}$$

✍ **Find each quotient.**

10) $5.2 \div 1.5$

11) $32.6 \div 2.6$

12) $16.8 \div 6.2$

13) $4.7 \div 7.7$

14) $99 \div 10$

15) $3.2 \div 100$

16) $66.3 \div 100$

17) $21.7 \div 10$

18) $3.9 \div 1000$

19) $4.2 \div 100$

20) $4.8 \div 2.2$

21) $0.2 \div 100$

Converting Between Fractions, Decimals and Mixed Numbers

✎ Convert fractions to decimals.

1) $\dfrac{21}{100}$

4) $\dfrac{4}{9}$

7) $\dfrac{9}{10}$

2) $\dfrac{46}{10}$

5) $\dfrac{3}{6}$

8) $\dfrac{11}{16}$

3) $\dfrac{9}{7}$

6) $\dfrac{50}{70}$

9) $\dfrac{21}{10}$

✎ Convert decimal into fraction or mixed numbers.

10) 0.8

17) 0.36

11) 4.4

18) 0.7

12) 3.6

19) 0.48

13) 2.2

20) 8.2

14) 0.12

21) 2.8

15) 0.2

22) 1.7

16) 0.07

23) 0.002

Answers of Worksheets – Chapter 2

Factoring Numbers

1) 1, 2, 3, 6, 9, 18, 27, 54

2) 1, 2, 4, 5, 8, 10, 16, 20, 40, 80

3) 1, 2, 29, 58

4) 1, 3, 13, 39

5) 1, 2, 3, 4, 6, 8, 9, 12, 18, 24, 36, 72

6) 1, 3, 9, 11, 33, 99

7) 1, 2, 4, 19, 38, 76

8) 1, 2, 7, 14

9) 1, 2, 4, 13, 26, 52

10) 1, 43

11) 1, 2, 31, 62

12) 1, 3, 5, 15, 25, 75

13) 1, 3, 11, 33

14) 1, 2, 3, 4, 5, 6, 10, 12, 15, 20, 30, 60

15) 1, 17

16) $2 \times 2 \times 5$

17) $3 \times 3 \times 5$

18) 3×17

19) 5×19

20) $2 \times 2 \times 2 \times 2 \times 2$

21) $2 \times 2 \times 2 \times 2 \times 3$

22) $2 \times 2 \times 2 \times 2 \times 2 \times 2$

23) 2×11

24) $2 \times 2 \times 2 \times 11$

25) $2 \times 2 \times 2 \times 2$

26) $2 \times 2 \times 2 \times 5$

27) $2 \times 2 \times 3$

28) $7 \times 3 \times 3$

29) $3 \times 2 \times 3$

30) 2×17

Greatest Common Factor

1) 10
2) 2
3) 5
4) 1
5) 5
6) 15
7) 6
8) 7
9) 8
10) 1
11) 5
12) 6
13) 6
14) 10
15) 18
16) 5
17) 7
18) 2
19) 25
20) 7
21) 5
22) 6
23) 12
24) 8

Least Common Multiple

1) 16
2) 57
3) 42
4) 24
5) 24
6) 360
7) 30
8) 63
9) 323
10) 72
11) 55
12) 117
13) 12
14) 48
15) 60
16) 210
17) 96
18) 180
19) 84
20) 24
21) 42
22) 2,952
23) 36
24) 1,560

PSSA Math Workbook – Grade 7

Divisibility Rules

1) 14   **2** 3 4 5 6 **7** 8 9 10
2) 80   **2** 3 **4** **5** 6 7 **8** 9 **10**
3) 28   **2** 3 **4** 5 6 **7** 8 9 10
4) 30   **2** **3** 4 **5** **6** 7 8 9 **10**
5) 44   **2** 3 **4** 5 6 7 8 9 10
6) 52   **2** 3 **4** 5 6 7 8 9 10
7) 25   2 3 4 **5** 6 7 8 9 10
8) 75   2 **3** 4 **5** 6 7 8 9 10
9) 36   **2** **3** **4** 5 **6** 7 8 **9** 10
10) 48 **2** **3** 4 5 **6** 7 **8** 9 10
11) 72 **2** **3** **4** 5 **6** 7 **8** **9** 10
12) 180   **2** **3** **4** **5** **6** 7 8 **9** **10**

Simplifying Fractions.

1) $\frac{1}{2}$

2) $\frac{1}{2}$

3) $\frac{1}{4}$

4) $\frac{3}{2}$

5) $\frac{1}{6}$

6) $\frac{1}{7}$

7) $\frac{1}{4}$

8) $\frac{3}{5}$

9) $\frac{1}{3}$

10) $\frac{1}{8}$

11) $\frac{7}{27}$

12) $\frac{2}{3}$

13) $\frac{5}{9}$

14) $\frac{1}{2}$

15) $\frac{1}{3}$

16) $\frac{3}{8}$

17) $\frac{4}{9}$

18) $\frac{1}{2}$

19) $\frac{1}{7}$

20) $\frac{1}{10}$

21) $\frac{1}{2}$

22) $\frac{4}{3}$

23) $\frac{1}{3}$

24) $\frac{11}{12}$

Adding and Subtracting Fractions

1) $\frac{16}{21}$

2) $\frac{26}{15}$

3) $\frac{7}{8}$

4) $\frac{11}{12}$

5) 1

6) $\frac{41}{42}$

7) $\frac{37}{20}$

8) $\frac{29}{35}$

9) $\frac{26}{21}$

10) $\frac{11}{3}$

11) $\frac{5}{12}$ 14) $\frac{5}{8}$ 17) $\frac{1}{2}$

12) $\frac{1}{8}$ 15) $\frac{2}{3}$ 18) $\frac{4}{9}$

13) $\frac{1}{10}$ 16) $\frac{5}{21}$

Multiplying and Dividing Fractions

1) $\frac{5}{21}$ 8) $\frac{1}{6}$ 15) $\frac{10}{7}$

2) $\frac{6}{35}$ 9) $\frac{3}{8}$ 16) $\frac{1}{3}$

3) $\frac{15}{28}$ 10) $\frac{7}{9}$ 17) 4

4) $\frac{3}{7}$ 11) 10   18) 2

5) $\frac{5}{44}$ 12) $\frac{1}{4}$ 19) $\frac{2}{3}$

6) $\frac{2}{45}$ 13) $\frac{3}{2}$

7) $\frac{21}{20}$ 14) $\frac{11}{4}$

Adding Mixed Numbers

1) 11   5) $5\frac{3}{7}$ 9) $5\frac{6}{7}$

2) 9   6) 11   10) $8\frac{1}{3}$

3) $9\frac{1}{3}$ 7) $6\frac{10}{11}$ 11) $4\frac{1}{5}$

4) 7   8) 4   12) $6\frac{5}{6}$

Subtract Mixed Numbers

1) 2   5) $2\frac{1}{2}$ 9) $2\frac{1}{7}$

2) $1\frac{1}{7}$ 6) $3\frac{1}{5}$ 10) $4\frac{3}{5}$

3) $4\frac{1}{9}$ 7) $1\frac{1}{9}$ 11) $2\frac{1}{3}$

4) $1\frac{1}{2}$ 8) 1   12) 1

Multiplying Mixed Numbers

1) $3\frac{1}{9}$ 4) $8\frac{8}{15}$ 7) $5\frac{15}{16}$

2) $5\frac{7}{25}$ 5) $11\frac{1}{12}$ 8) $7\frac{12}{25}$

3) $5\frac{5}{6}$ 6) $3\frac{1}{2}$ 9) 18

10) $10\frac{2}{15}$ 11) $5\frac{5}{12}$ 12) $5\frac{2}{3}$

Dividing Mixed Numbers

1) $\frac{5}{6}$ 7) $2\frac{41}{72}$ 13) $\frac{63}{76}$

2) $2\frac{4}{15}$ 8) $\frac{6}{7}$ 14) $1\frac{9}{56}$

3) $3\frac{19}{45}$ 9) $1\frac{23}{72}$ 15) $\frac{72}{95}$

4) $2\frac{1}{25}$ 10) $1\frac{53}{133}$ 16) $3\frac{4}{11}$

5) $1\frac{7}{18}$ 11) $2\frac{9}{28}$

6) $2\frac{2}{15}$ 12) 2

Comparing Decimals

1) $2.26 < 2.29$ 9) $10 > 0.99$ 17) $8.32 > 0.832$

2) $1.5 > 0.75$ 10) $6.65 > 0.995$ 18) $0.13 > 0.013$

3) $5.1 = 5.1$ 11) $2.43 < 2.45$ 19) $63.7 = 63.7$

4) $6.48 < 64.8$ 12) $6.66 < 6.67$ 20) $0.03 < 0.30$

5) $3.95 > 0.395$ 13) $8.08 < 8.12$ 21) $0.59 < 0.6$

6) $8.2 > 8$ 14) $1.11 > 0.111$ 22) $0.7 > 0.07$

7) $9.1 > 0.96$ 15) $5.8 > 8.76$ 23) $0.80 = 0.8$

8) $4.13 > 0.813$ 16) $3.32 < 3.37$ 24) $0.46 < 0.54$

Rounding Decimals

1) 0.2 9) 1.93 17) 75.8

2) 3.0 10) 7.4 18) 636

3) 6.6 11) 2 19) 16

4) 0.3 12) 5 20) 86

5) 6 13) 6.9 21) 2

6) 0.9 14) 8.5 22) 86

7) 8.2 15) 91 23) 116.5

8) 7 16) 86 24) 8.1

Adding and Subtracting Decimals

1) 0.98 3) 77.81 5) 117.34

2) 119.63 4) 10.73 6) 21.39

7) 4.6   10) 12.1   13) 12.6

8) 9.3   11) 5.3   14) 10

9) 7.1   12) 10

Multiplying and Dividing Decimals

1) 2.88   8) 9715   15) 0.032

2) 9.9   9) 29980   16) 0.663

3) 3.64   10) 3.466…   17) 2.17

4) 26.46   11) 12.5384…   18) 0.0039

5) 141.12   12) 2.7096…   19) 0.042

6) 7.98   13) 0.6103…   20) 2.18…

7) 7.7   14) 9.9   21) 0.002

Converting Between Fractions, Decimals and Mixed Numbers

1) 0.21   10) $\frac{4}{5}$ 17) $\frac{9}{25}$

2) 4.6   11) $4\frac{2}{5}$ 18) $\frac{7}{10}$

3) 1.2857…

4) 0.4444…   12) $3\frac{3}{5}$ 19) $\frac{12}{25}$

5) 0.5   13) $2\frac{1}{5}$ 20) $8\frac{1}{5}$

6) 0.7142…   14) $\frac{3}{25}$ 21) $2\frac{4}{5}$

7) 0.9

8) 0.6875…   15) $\frac{1}{5}$ 22) $1\frac{4}{6}$

9) 2.1   16) $\frac{7}{100}$ 23) $\frac{2}{1000}$

Chapter 3: Percent

Topics that you'll learn in this chapter:

✓ Percentage Calculations

✓ Converting Between Percent, Fractions, and Decimals

✓ Percent Problems

✓ Find What Percentage a Number Is of Another

✓ Find a Percentage of a Given Number

✓ Percent of Increase and Decrease

Percentage Calculations

🖎Calculate the percentages.

1) 35% of 10

2) 80% of 40

3) 55% of 60

4) 70% of 65

5) 85% of 20

6) 70% of 0

7) 65% of 7

8) 97% of 45

9) 50% of 160

10) 40% of 80

11) 70% of 70

12) 85% of 60

13) 30% of 90

14) 75% of 120

15) 80% of 10

16) 60% of 880

17) 65% of 950

18) 45% of 180

🖎*Solve.*

19) 60 is what percentage of 200?

20) What percentage of 500 is 50

21) Find what percentage of 800 is 500.

22) 45 is what percentage of 90?

Converting Between Percent, Fractions, and Decimals

✎ **Converting fractions to decimals.**

1) $\dfrac{85}{100}$

4) $\dfrac{75}{100}$

7) $\dfrac{89}{100}$

2) $\dfrac{48}{100}$

5) $\dfrac{8}{100}$

8) $\dfrac{45}{100}$

3) $\dfrac{3}{5}$

6) $\dfrac{12}{30}$

9) $\dfrac{1}{25}$

✎ **Write each decimal as a percent.**

10) 0.85

13) 0.958

16) 8.49

11) 0.79

14) 0.25

17) 0.0012

12) 0.032

15) 0.049

18) 6.98

✎ **Converting fractions to percent.**

19) $\dfrac{2}{25}$

21) $\dfrac{5}{18}$

23) $\dfrac{11}{50}$

20) $\dfrac{1}{5}$

22) $\dfrac{2}{7}$

24) $\dfrac{2}{5}$

Percent Problems

Solve each problem.

1) 50 is 250% of what?

2) 98% of what number is 70?

3) 46% of 126 is what number?

4) What percent of 165 is 34.9?

5) 90 is what percent of 225?

6) 89 is 98% of what?

7) 85 is 15% of what?

8) 44% of 98 is what?

9) 2 is what percent of 72.2?

10) What is 83% of 24 m?

11) What is 50% of 280 inches?

12) 25inches is 65% of what?

13) 70% of 95 hours is what?

14) What percent of 65.2 is 36?

15) Joe scored 25 out of 38 marks in Algebra, 37 out of 52 marks in science and 25 out of 28 marks in mathematics. In which subject his percentage of marks is best?

16) Ella require 50% to pass. If she gets 420 marks and falls short by 30 marks, what were the maximum marks she could have got?

Percentage of Numbers

✎ **Find the percentage of numbers.**

1) 5 is what percent of 50?

2) 35 is what percent of 70?

3) 90 is what percent of 900?

4) 36 is what percent of 120?

5) 8 is what percent of 40?

6) 24 is what percent of 240?

7) 24 is what percent of 48?

8) 30 is what percent of 120?

9) 0.9 is what percent of 2?

10) 120 is what percent of 60?

11) 18 is what percent of 72?

12) 12 is what percent of 24?

13) 30 is what percent of 150?

14) 120 is what percent of 150?

15) 7000 is what percent of 1000?

16) 800 is what percent of 40,000?

17) 80 is what percent of 1600?

18) 240 is what percent of 400?

19) 30 is what percent of 20?

20) 2.8 is what percent of 140?

Percentage of a Given Numbers

✎ **Find a Percentage of a Given Number.**

1) 100% of 9	7) 80% of 2	13) 70% of 12
2) 40% of 20	8) 45% of 90	14) 8% of 4
3) 30% of 30	9) 20% of 60	15) 48% of 60
4) 65% of 40	10) 24% of 180	16) 36% of 160
5) 21% of 60	11) 90% 0f 240	17) 91% of 3
6) 50% of 0	12) 10% of 210	18) 25% of 30

Percent of Increase and Decrease

✎ **Find each percent change to the nearest percent. Increase or decrease.**

1) From 98grams to 94 grams.	5) From 200 ft to 199 ft
2) From 65 m to 165 m	6) From 240 inches to 280 inches
3) From $120 to $60	7) From 2 ft to 4 ft
4) From 143 ft to 128ft	8) From 93 miles to 3miles

9) A number is increased by 20 % and then decreased by 20 %. Find the net increase or decrease per cent?

10) The price of wheat increased by 20 %. By how much per cent should mother reduce her consumption in the house so that her expenditure on wheat does not increase?

Answers of Worksheets – Chapter 3

Percentage Calculations

1) 3.5	9) 80	17) 617.5
2) 32	10) 32	18) 81
3) 33	11) 49	19) 30%
4) 45.5	12) 51	20) 10%
5) 17	13) 27	21) 62.5%
6) 0	14) 90	22) 50%
7) 4.55	15) 8	
8) 43.65	16) 528	

Converting Between Percent, Fractions, and Decimals

1) 0.85	9) 0.04	17) 0.12%
2) 0.48	10) 85%	18) 698%
3) 0.6	11) 79%	19) 8%
4) 0.75	12) 3.2%	20) 20%
5) 0.08	13) 95.8%	21) 27.78%
6) 0.4	14) 25%	22) 28.57%
7) 0.89	15) 4.9%	23) 22%
8) 0.45	16) 849%	24) 40%

Percent Problems

1) 20	7) 560	13) 135.7 hours
2) 71.43	8) 222.73	14) 55.21%
3) 57.96	9) 2.77%	15) Mathematic
4) 21.15%	10) 28.9m	16) 900
5) 40%	11) 560 inches	
6) 90.82	12) 38.46inches	

Percentage of The Number

1) 10 %	5) 20 %	9) 45 %
2) 50 %	6) 10 %	10) 200 %
3) 5 %	7) 50 %	11) 25 %
4) 30 %	8) 25%	12) 50%

13) 20 %

14) 80 %

15) 700%

16) 2%

17) 5 %

18) 60 %

19) 150%

20) 2 %

Percentage of Given Numbers

1) 9

2) 8

3) 9

4) 26

5) 12.6

6) 0

7) 1.6

8) 40.5

9) 12

10) 43.2

11) 216

12) 21

13) 8.4

14) 0.32

15) 28.8

16) 57.6

17) 2.73

18) 7.5

Percent of Increase and Decrease

1) 4.08% decrease

2) 153.85% increase

3) 50% decrease

4) 10.5% decrease

5) 0.5% decrease

6) 16.67% increase

7) 100% increase

8) 96.77% decrease

9) 4% decrease

10) $16\frac{2}{3}\%$

Chapter 4: Proportions and Ratios

Topics that you'll learn in this chapter:

✓ Writing Ratios

✓ Simplifying Ratios

✓ Proportional Ratios

✓ Create a Proportion

✓ Similar Figures

✓ Similar Figure Word Problems

✓ Ratio and Rates Word Problems

Writing Ratios

Express each ratio as a rate and unite rate.

1) 250 miles on 5 gallons of gas.

2) 32 dollars for 4 books.

3) 100 miles on 4 gallons of gas

4) 56 inches of snow in 8 hours

Express each ratio as a fraction in the simplest form.

5) 4 feet out of 24 feet

6) 6 cakes out of 32 cakes

7) 9 dimes t0 15 dimes

8) 7 dimes out of 35 coins

9) 10 cups to 100 cups

10) 36 gallons to 99 gallons

11) 60 miles out of 90 miles

12) 14 blue cars out of 28 cars

13) 11 pennies to 110 pennies

14) 54 beetles out of 63 insects

Proportional Ratios

✎ **Solve each proportion.**

1) $\dfrac{3}{6} = \dfrac{3}{d}$

2) $\dfrac{k}{6} = \dfrac{27}{18}$

3) $\dfrac{30}{6} = \dfrac{15}{x}$

4) $\dfrac{x}{72} = \dfrac{1}{9}$

5) $\dfrac{d}{8} = \dfrac{4}{32}$

6) $\dfrac{22}{4} = \dfrac{33}{x}$

7) $\dfrac{6}{24} = \dfrac{k}{72}$

8) $\dfrac{25}{5} = \dfrac{5}{d}$

9) $\dfrac{x}{6} = \dfrac{12}{9}$

10) $\dfrac{21}{4} = \dfrac{x}{12}$

11) $\dfrac{16}{x} = \dfrac{6}{3}$

12) $\dfrac{x}{3} = \dfrac{15}{5}$

13) $\dfrac{30}{10} = \dfrac{k}{30}$

14) $\dfrac{16}{4} = \dfrac{4}{d}$

15) $\dfrac{x}{2} = \dfrac{49}{7}$

16) $\dfrac{4}{12} = \dfrac{k}{18}$

17) $\dfrac{24}{18} = \dfrac{8}{d}$

18) $\dfrac{10}{x} = \dfrac{20}{40}$

19) $\dfrac{d}{5} = \dfrac{5}{10}$

20) $\dfrac{k}{2} = \dfrac{16}{4}$

21) $\dfrac{4}{5} = \dfrac{x}{10}$

Simplifying Ratios

✍ Reduce each ratio.

1) 12 : 18	9) 24 : 48	17) 3 : 93
2) 25 : 50	10) 9 : 99	18) 17 : 34
3) 2 : 12	11) 129 : 90	19) 2 : 50
4) 2 : 20	12) 15 : 60	20) 6 : 42
5) 6 : 54	13) 21 : 63	21) 11 : 33
6) 24 : 3	14) 60 : 10	22) 12 : 28
7) 15 : 5	15) 5 : 100	23) 88 : 44
8) 48 : 54	16) 13 : 195	24) 77 : 110

Create a Proportion

✍ Create proportion from the given set of numbers.

1) 10, 2, 5, 25	7) 49, 7, 42, 6
2) 8, 4, 2, 1	8) 2, 3, 20, 30
3) 5, 30, 42, 7	9) 2, 4, 6, 12
4) 32, 5, 40, 4	10) 9, 45, 15, 3
5) 3, 4, 27, 36	11) 12, 240, 13, 260
6) 14, 7, 18, 9	12) 6, 5, 20, 24

Similar Figures

✎ **Each pair of figures is similar. Find the missing side.**

1)

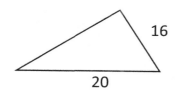

2)

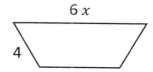

3)

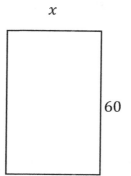

Similar Figure Word Problems

✍Answer each question and round your answer to the nearest whole number.

1) If a 32.6 ft tall flagpole casts a 158.2 ft long shadow, then how long is the shadow that a 5.8 ft tall woman casts?

2) A model igloo has a scale of 1 in:4 ft. If the real igloo is 24 ft wide, then how wide is the model igloo?

3) If a 42 ft tall tree casts a 7 ft long shadow, then how tall is an adult giraffe that casts a 2 ft shadow?

4) Find the distance between San Joe and Mount Pleasant if they are 7cm apart on a map with a scale of 1 cm: 7 km.

5) A telephone booth that is 28 ft tall casts a shadow that is 14 ft long. Find the height of a lawn ornament that casts a 9 ft shadow.

Ratio and Rates Word Problems

Solve.

1) In a party, 20 soft drinks are required for every 12 guests. If there are120 guests, how many soft drinks is required?

2) In Jack's class, 8 of the students are tall and 32 are short. In Michael's class 18 students are tall and 10 students are short. Which class has a higher ratio of tall to short students?

3) Are these ratios equivalent?

   18 cards to 36 animals 9 marbles to 18 people.

4) The price of 5 apples at the Quick Market is $2.15. The price of 6 of the same apples at Walmart is $3.25. Which place is the better buy?

5) The bakers at a Bakery can make 150 bagels in 5 hours. How many bagels can they bake in 12hours? What is that rate per hour?

6) You can buy 6 cans of green beans at a supermarket for $5.4. How much does it cost to buy 50 cans of green beans?

Answers of Worksheets – Chapter 4

Writing Ratios

1) $\frac{250 \text{ miles}}{5 \text{ gallons}}$, 50 miles per gallon

2) $\frac{32 \text{ dollars}}{4 \text{ books}}$, 8.00 dollars per book

3) $\frac{100 \text{ miles}}{4 \text{ gallons}}$, 25 miles per gallon

4) $\frac{56" \text{ of snow}}{8 \text{ hours}}$, 7 inches of snow per hour

5) $\frac{1}{6}$ 9) $\frac{1}{10}$ 13) $\frac{1}{10}$

6) $\frac{3}{16}$ 10) $\frac{4}{11}$ 14) $\frac{6}{7}$

7) $\frac{3}{5}$ 11) $\frac{2}{3}$

8) $\frac{1}{5}$ 12) $\frac{1}{2}$

Proportional Ratios

1) 6   8) 1   15) 14
2) 9   9) 8   16) 6
3) 3   10) 63   17) 6
4) 8   11) 8   18) 20
5) 1   12) 9   19) 2.5
6) 6   13) 90   20) 8
7) 18   14) 1   21) 8

Simplifying Ratios

1) 2: 3   9) 1: 2   17) 1: 31
2) 1: 2   10) 1: 11   18) 1: 2
3) 1: 6   11) 43: 30   19) 1: 25
4) 1: 10   12) 1: 4   20) 1: 7
5) 1: 9   13) 1: 3   21) 1: 3
6) 8: 1   14) 6: 1   22) 3: 7
7) 3: 1   15) 1: 20   23) 2: 1
8) 8: 9   16) 1: 15   24) 7: 10

Create a Proportion

1) $10: 2 = 25: 5$

2) $1: 4 = 2: 8$

3) $5: 7 = 30: 42$

4) $4: 5 = 32: 40$

5) $3: 4 = 27: 36$

6) $14: 7 = 18: 9$

7) $6: 7 = 42: 49$

8) $2: 3 = 20: 30$

9) $4: 2 = 12: 6$

10) $45: 9 = 15: 3$

11) $12: 240 = 13: 260$

12) $6: 5 = 24: 20$

Similar Figures

1) 5

2) 4

3) 15

Similar Figure Word Problems

1) 28.146 ft

2) 6 in

3) 12 ft

4) 49 km

5) 18 ft

Ratio and Rates Word Problems

1) 200

2) The ratio of Michael's class is higher.

3) Yes! Both ratios are 1 to 2

4) The price at the Quick Market is a better buy.

5) 360, the rate is 30 per hour.

6) $45

Chapter 5: Exponents and Radicals

Topics that you'll learn in this chapter:

- ✓ Multiplication Property of Exponents

- ✓ Division Property of Exponents

- ✓ Powers of Products and Quotients

- ✓ Zero, Negative Exponents and Bases

Multiplication Property of Exponents

✎ **Simplify.**

1) $4^3 \times 4^2$

2) $2 \cdot 2^2 \cdot 2^3$

3) $2^4 \cdot 2$

4) $8x^2 \cdot x$

5) $15x^7 \cdot x$

6) $3x \cdot x^3$

7) $2x^5 \cdot 5x^4$

8) $5x^2 \cdot 3x^2y^2$

9) $6y^5 \cdot 8xy^2$

10) $5xy^3 \cdot 4x^3y^2$

11) $(2x^3)^2$

12) $2x^4y \cdot 3x^2y^2$

13) $6x \cdot 5y^4x^2 \cdot 2yx^3$

14) $(x^3)^3$

15) $(3x^2)^3$

16) $2x^3y^5 \cdot 2xy^2$

Division Property of Exponents

✎ **Simplify.**

1) $\dfrac{4^3}{4}$

2) $\dfrac{51}{51^{14}}$

3) $\dfrac{5^2}{5^3}$

4) $\dfrac{3^4}{3^1}$

5) $\dfrac{x}{x^7}$

6) $\dfrac{42x^2}{6x^2}$

7) $\dfrac{3x^{-3}}{12x^{-1}}$

8) $\dfrac{81x^5}{9x^3}$

9) $\dfrac{3x^4}{4x^5}$

10) $\frac{21x}{3x^2}$

11) $\frac{3x}{7x^4}$

12) $\frac{2x^2}{3x^6}$

13) $\frac{18x^3}{10x^5}$

14) $\frac{14x}{7y^5}$

15) $\frac{2xy^5}{x^5y}$

16) $\frac{2x^2}{5x}$

17) $\frac{8x^2y}{x^3}$

18) $\frac{3x^4}{7x^5y^4}$

19) $\frac{yx^3}{5yx^3}$

20) $\frac{3x^4}{2x^5}$

21) $\frac{x^7}{3x^7}$

Powers of Products and Quotients

Simplify.

1) $(2x^2)^3$

2) $(xy)^2$

3) $(5x^3)^2$

4) $(9x^3)^2$

5) $(4x^2y^3)^2$

6) $(5x^2y^3)^2$

7) $(2xy^2)^3$

8) $(2x^3y)^4$

9) $(7x^4y^8)^2$

10) $(10x)^3$

11) $(x^5)^3$

12) $(8x^{10}y^2)^3$

13) $(9x^2x^2)^2$

14) $(2x^2\,8x)^2$

15) $(11x^9y^3)^2$

16) $(6x^5\,y^3)^2$

17) $(3\,x^3\,)^5$

18) $(7x^3)^2$

19) $(2x\,4y^4)^2$

20) $(6xy)^3$

21) $(15x^2y^3)^2$

Zero and Negative Exponents

🖎 Evaluate the following expressions.

1) 4^{-2}

2) 5^{-2}

3) 6^{-2}

4) 3^{-4}

5) 10^{-1}

6) 33^{-1}

7) 6^{-1}

8) 3^{-2}

9) 9^{-2}

10) 4^{-1}

11) 5^{-3}

12) 2^{-5}

13) 11^{-2}

14) 2^{-4}

15) 7^{-2}

16) 2^{-3}

17) 2^{-2}

18) 9^{-1}

19) 4^{-3}

20) 10^{-4}

21) $\left(\frac{2}{3}\right)^{-2}$

22) $\left(\frac{1}{3}\right)^{-2}$

23) $\left(\frac{1}{2}\right)^{-3}$

24) $\left(\frac{6}{5}\right)^{-2}$

25) 11^{-2}

26) 3^{-1}

Negative Exponents and Negative Bases

🖎 Simplify.

1) 7^{-1}

2) $-2x^{-2}$

3) $\frac{x}{x^{-5}}$

4) $-\frac{a^{-2}}{b^{-1}}$

5) $\frac{7}{x^{-5}}$

6) $\frac{2b}{-5c^{-2}}$

7) $\frac{2n^{-1}}{12p^{-2}}$

8) $\frac{8b^{-4}}{3c^{-2}}$

9) $89xy^{-2}$

10) $\left(\frac{1}{3}\right)^{-2}$

11) $\left(\frac{6}{7}\right)^{-2}$

12) $\left(\frac{x}{4yz}\right)^{-2}$

Writing Scientific Notation

✍ **Write each number in scientific notation.**

1) 25×10^3	7) 0.0076	13) 0.108
2) 12	8) 2900	14) 20
3) 0.0015	9) 100,000	15) 260
4) 54,000	10) 3,600,000	16) 1,000,000
5) 0.0051	11) 60,000,000	17) 0.00015
6) 666	12) 150	18) 0.3

Square Roots

✍ **Find the value each square root.**

1) $\sqrt{25}$	8) $\sqrt{16}$	15) $\sqrt{961}$
2) $\sqrt{1,600}$	9) $\sqrt{64}$	16) $\sqrt{400}$
3) $\sqrt{100}$	10) $\sqrt{36}$	17) $\sqrt{1}$
4) $\sqrt{121}$	11) $\sqrt{484}$	18) $\sqrt{196}$
5) $\sqrt{4}$	12) $\sqrt{49}$	19) $\sqrt{144}$
6) $\sqrt{225}$	13) $\sqrt{0.01}$	20) $\sqrt{169}$
7) $\sqrt{10,000}$	14) $\sqrt{81}$	21) $\sqrt{676}$

Answers of Worksheets – Chapter 5

Multiplication Property of Exponents

1) 4^5
2) 2^6
3) 2^5
4) $8x^3$
5) $15x^8$
6) $3x^4$

7) $10x^9$
8) $15x^4y^2$
9) $48xy^7$
10) $20x^4y^5$
11) $4x^6$
12) $6x^6y^3$

13) $60x^6y^5$
14) x^9
15) $27x^6$
16) $4x^4y^7$

Division Property of Exponents

1) 4^2
2) $\frac{1}{51^{13}}$
3) $\frac{1}{5}$
4) 3^3
5) $\frac{1}{x^6}$
6) 7
7) $\frac{1}{4x^2}$
8) $9x^2$

9) $\frac{3}{4x}$
10) $\frac{7}{x}$
11) $\frac{3}{7x^3}$
12) $\frac{2}{3x^4}$
13) $\frac{9}{5x^2}$
14) $\frac{2x}{y^5}$
15) $\frac{2y^4}{x^4}$

16) $\frac{2x}{5}$
17) $\frac{8y}{x}$
18) $\frac{3}{7xy^4}$
19) $\frac{1}{5}$
20) $\frac{3}{2x}$
21) $\frac{1}{3}$

Powers of Products and Quotients

1) $8x^6$
2) x^2y^2
3) $25x^6$
4) $81x^6$
5) $16x^4y^6$
6) $25x^4y^6$
7) $8x^3y^6$

8) $8x^{12}y^4$
9) $49x^8y^{16}$
10) $1,000x^3$
11) x^{15}
12) $512x^{30}y^6$
13) $81x^8$
14) $256x^6$

15) $121x^{18}y^6$
16) $36x^{10}y^6$
17) $243x^{15}$
18) $49x^6$
19) $64x^2y^8$
20) $216x^3y^3$
21) $225x^4y^6$

Zero and Negative Exponents

1) $\frac{1}{16}$
2) $\frac{1}{25}$

3) $\frac{1}{36}$
4) $\frac{1}{81}$

5) $\frac{1}{10}$
6) $\frac{1}{33}$

7) $\frac{1}{6}$

8) $\frac{1}{9}$

9) $\frac{1}{81}$

10) $\frac{1}{4}$

11) $\frac{1}{125}$

12) $\frac{1}{32}$

13) $\frac{1}{121}$

14) $\frac{1}{16}$

15) $\frac{1}{49}$

16) $\frac{1}{8}$

17) $\frac{1}{4}$

18) $\frac{1}{9}$

19) $\frac{1}{64}$

20) $\frac{1}{10,000}$

21) $\frac{9}{4}$

22) 9

23) 8

24) $\frac{25}{36}$

25) $\frac{1}{121}$

26) $\frac{1}{3}$

Negative Exponents and Negative Bases

1) $\frac{1}{7}$

2) $-\frac{2}{x^2}$

3) x^5

4) $-\frac{b^1}{a^2}$

5) $7x^5$

6) $-2\frac{bc^2}{5}$

7) $\frac{p^2}{6n}$

8) $\frac{8c^2}{3b^4}$

9) $\frac{89x}{y^2}$

10) 9

11) $\frac{49}{36}$

12) $\frac{16y^2z^2}{x^2}$

Writing Scientific Notation

1) 2.5×10^4

2) 1.2×10^1

3) 1.5×10^{-3}

4) 5.4×10^4

5) 5.1×10^{-3}

6) 6.66×10^2

7) 7.6×10^{-3}

8) 2.9×10^3

9) 1×10^5

10) 3.6×10^6

11) 6×10^7

12) 1.5×10^2

13) 1.08×10^{-1}

14) 2×10^1

15) 2.6×10^2

16) 1×10^6

17) 1.5×10^{-4}

18) 3×10^{-1}

Square Roots

1) 5

2) 40

3) 10

4) 11

5) 2

6) 15

7) 100

8) 4

9) 8

10) 6

11) 22

12) 7

13) 0.1

14) 9

15) 31

16) 20

17) 1

18) 14

19) 12

20) 13

21) 26

Chapter 6: Algebraic Expressions

Topics that you'll learn in this chapter:

- ✓ Find a Rule between input and output

- ✓ Variables and Expressions

- ✓ Translate Phrases

- ✓ The Distributive Property

- ✓ Simplifying Variable Expressions

- ✓ Evaluating One Variable

- ✓ Evaluating Two Variables

Find a Rule

✎ **Complete the output.**

1- **Rule:** the output is $x + 25$

Input	x	8	15	20	38	40
Output	y					

2- **Rule:** the output is $x \times 18$

Input	x	3	7	10	11	15
Output	y					

3- **Rule:** the output is $x \div 7$

Input	x	126	147	105	280	455
Output	y					

✎ **Find a rule to write an expression.**

4- **Rule:** _____

Input	x	11	13	15	20
Output	y	55	65	75	100

5- **Rule:** _____

Input	x	10	28	32	46
Output	y	14	32	36	50

6- **Rule:** _____

Input	x	84	132	180	252
Output	y	14	22	30	42

Variables and Expressions

✍ **Write a verbal expression for each algebraic expression.**

1) $2a - 4b$

2) $8c^2 + 2d$

3) $x - 8$

4) $\dfrac{80}{15}$

5) $a^2 + b^3$

6) $2x + 4$

7) $x^2 - 10y + 8$

8) $x^3 + 9y^2 - 4$

9) $\dfrac{1}{3} x + \dfrac{3}{4} y - 6$

10) $\dfrac{1}{5} (x + 8) - 10y$

✍ **Write an algebraic expression for each verbal expression.**

11) 9 less than h

12) The product of 9 and b

13) The 26 divided by k

14) The product of 5 and the third power of x

15) 10 more than h to the fifth power

16) 20 more than twice d

17) One fourth the square of b

18) The difference of 23 and 4 times a number

19) 60 more than the cube of a number

20) Three-quarters the cube of a number

Translate Phrases

✎ **Write an algebraic expression for each phrase.**

1) A number increased by sixty–one.

2) The sum of twenty and 2 times a number

3) The difference between fifty–seven and a number.

4) The quotient of twenty-two and a number.

5) Twice a number decreased by 50.

6) four times the sum of a number and – 20.

7) A number divided by – 12.

8) The quotient of 49 and the product of a number and – 12.

9) ten subtracted from 2 times a number.

10)   The difference of eight and a number.

Expressions and Variables

✏️Simplify each expression.

1) $2x + 4x,$

     use $x = 5$

2) $10(-2x + 5) + 7,$

     use $x = 3$

3) $12x - 5x + 9 - 6,$

     use $x = 1$

4) $5x + 6x - 15,$

     use $x = 4$

5) $(-4)(-2x - 6y),$

     use $x = 3, y = 1$

6) $8x + 13 - 5y,$

     use $x = 5, y = 6$

7) $(-6)(-10x + 14y),$

     use $x = 3, y = 3$

8) $15x + 13y,$

     use $x = 2, y = 1$

Distributive Property

✏️Use the distributive property to simply each expression.

1) $(-2)(2x - 1)$

2) $-3(4 + 8x)$

3) $3(10 + 8x)$

4) $(-9x + 1)2$

5) $(14 - 6x)(-2)$

6) $(-15)(2x + 6)$

7) $(-5x)(-2 + 3x) - 4x(2 - 1x)$

8) $(-10)(x + 3) - (2 - 6x)$

9) $(-30)(2x - 1) + 15(4x + 2)$

Simplifying Variables

✎ **Simplify each expression.**

1) $(-2x + 14)\,3$

2) $5 + 3x + 6x - 8$

3) $(-8) - (4)\,(2x + 3)$

4) $3x - 25x$

5) $3\,(3x + 2) + 9x$

6) $(-32x) - 15x$

7) $13x - 34 - 16x$

8) $(-43x) + 7x$

9) $4\,(1 + 6x) - 8x$

10) $(-12x) - (2 - 2x)$

11) $4\,(2x - 3) + 12x$

12) $35x + 17 + 20x$

13) $(-4x) - 18 + 24x$

14) $(-7\,x) + 6x$

15) $(-35x) + 43 + 36x$

16) $(-23x) - 17 + 13$

17) $9 - 3x^2 - 7x^2$

18) $11 + 22\,x^2 + 9$

19) $41x^2 - 30\,x^2 + 24x$

20) $31x^2 - 21x + 14x$

21) $24x + 6\,(12 - 4x)$

22) $18x + 30(-x - 1)$

23) $30\,(-2x - 1) - 5$

24) $4.5\,x \times (-20x)$

Evaluating One Variable

✍ **Simplify each algebraic expression.**

1) $19 - 5x$, $x = 3$

2) $3x + 12$, $x = 2$

3) $4x + 3$, $x = 5$

4) $3x + (-5)$, $x = -4$

5) $10x + 16$, $x = 1$

6) $24x - 16$, $x = -2$

7) $-10 + 20x - 6$, $x = 2$

8) $30 - 4x$, $x = 7$

9) $\frac{60}{x} - 5$, $x = 6$

10) $(-8) + \frac{x}{8} + 10x$, $x = 8$

11) $(-22) + \frac{x}{7}$, $x = 49$

12) $\left(-\frac{18}{x}\right) - 13 + x$, $x = 3$

13) $\left(-\frac{48}{x}\right) + 29 + 2x$, $x = 3$

14) $(-14) + \frac{x}{4}$, $x = 32$

15) $50(3x - 1)$, $x = -1$

16) $20x - 14x - 13 + 12$, $x = 2$

17) $\left(-\frac{24}{x}\right) + 1 + 15x$, $x = 4$

18) $20(4a + 10a)$, $a = 2$

19) $90 - 15x + 17 - 4x$, $x = 5$

20) $91x - 160 + 14x$, $x = 2$

21) $87 + 30(2x + x)$, $x = -1$

22) $10x + 6x - 13x$, $x = 2$

23) $2x \times 9 \div 3x$, $x = 3$

Evaluating Two Variables

✎ **Simplify each algebraic expression.**

1) $5x + 6y - 12 + 13,$

$x = 5, y = 3$

2) $(-\frac{36}{x}) + 17 + 2y,$

$x = 3, y = 5$

3) $(-3)(-22a + 33b),$

$a = 2, b = 1$

4) $60 - 30x + 28 - 24y,$

$x = 1, y = 1$

5) $16x + 20 - 13y,$

$x = 2, y = 2$

6) $44 - 2(-23x + 42y),$

$x = 5, y = 4$

7) $100x - 10y,$

$x = 2, y = 9$

8) $x \times 5 \div 10y,$

$x = 4, y = 1$

9) $16x + 12 - 14y,$

$x = 9, y = 10$

10) $14a - (29 - 3b),$

$a = 2, b = 7$

Answers of Worksheets – Chapter 6

Find a Rule

1)

Input	x	8	15	20	38	40
Output	y	33	40	45	63	**65**

2)

Input	x	3	7	10	11	15
Output	y	54	**126**	180	198	270

3)

Input	x	126	147	105	280	455
Output	y	18	21	**15**	40	65

4) $y = 5x$ 5) $y = x + 4$ 6) $y = x \div 6$

Variables and Expressions

1) 2 times a minus 4 times b

2) 8 times c squared plus 2 times d

3) a number minus 8

4) the quotient of 80 and 15

5) a squared plus b cubed

6) the product of 2 and x plus 4

7) x squared minus the product of 10 and y plus 8

8) x cubed plus the product of 9 and y squared minus 4

9) the sum of one–thirds of x and three–quarters of y, minus 6

10) one–fifth of the sum of x and 8 minus the product of 10 and y

11) $9 < h$

12) $9b$

13) $\frac{26}{K}$

14) $5x^3$

15) $10 > h^5$

16) $2d < 20$

17) $\frac{1}{4}b^2$

18) $23 - 4a$

19) $60 > a^3$

20) $\frac{3}{4}x^3$

Translate Phrases

1) $x + 61$

2) $20 + 2x$

3) $57 - x$

4) $\frac{22}{x}$

5) $2x - 50$

6) $4(x + (-20))$

7) $\frac{x}{-12}$

8) $\frac{49}{-12x}$

9) $2x - 10$

10) $8 - x$

Expressions and Variables

1) 30
2) –3
3) 10

4) 29
5) 48
6) 23

7) –72
8) 43

Distributive Property

1) $-4x + 2$
2) $-24x - 12$
3) $24x + 30$

4) $-18x + 2$
5) $12x - 28$
6) $-30x - 90$

7) $-11x^2 + 2x$
8) $-4x - 32$
9) 60

Simplifying Variable

1) $-6x + 42$
2) $9x - 3$
3) $-8x - 20$
4) $-22x$
5) $18x + 6$
6) $-47x$
7) $-3x - 34$
8) $-36x$

9) $16x + 4$
10) $-10x - 2$
11) $20x - 12$
12) $55x + 17$
13) $20x - 18$
14) $-x$
15) $x + 43$
16) $-23x - 4$

17) $-10x^2 + 9$
18) $22x^2 + 20$
19) $11x^2 + 24x$
20) $31x^2 - 7x$
21) 72
22) $-12x - 30$
23) $-60x - 35$
24) $-90x^2$

Evaluating One Variable

1) 4
2) 18
3) 23
4) –17
5) 26
6) –64

7) 24
8) 2
9) 5
10) 73
11) –15
12) –16

13) 19
14) –6
15) –200
16) 11
17) 55
18) 560

19) 12
20) 50
21) –3
22) 6
23) 6

Evaluating Two Variables

1) 44
2) 15
3) 33
4) 34

5) 26
6) –62
7) 110
8) 2

9) 16
10) 20

Chapter 7: Equations

Topics that you'll learn in this chapter:

- ✓ One–Step Equations

- ✓ One–Step Equation Word Problems

- ✓ Two–Step Equations

- ✓ Two–Step Equation Word Problems

- ✓ Multi–Step Equations

One–Step Equations

✍ **Solve each equation.**

1) $x + 14 = 26$

2) $29 = (-11) + x$

3) $4x = (-84)$

4) $(-81) = (-9x)$

5) $(-19) = 13 + x$

6) $-12 + x = (-34)$

7) $13x = (-169)$

8) $18 = x + 15$

9) $(-36) + x = (-20)$

10) $-5x = (-25)$

11) $x - 25 = (-46)$

12) $x - 3 = (-20)$

13) $(-32) = x - 24$

14) $36 = 3x$

15) $(-7x) = -35$

16) $(-77) = (-7x)$

17) $x - 35 = 10$

18) $12x = 120$

19) $63 = (-7x)$

20) $4x = 68$

One–Step Equation Word Problems

✍ Solve.

1) How many boxes of envelopes can you buy with $40 if one box costs $5?

2) After paying $8.15 for a salad, Riya has $61.53. How much money did she have before buying the salad?

3) How many packages of Tissues can you buy with $81 if one package costs $4.5?

4) Last week Joe ran 40 miles more than Harrison. Joe ran 78 miles. How many miles did Harrison run?

5) Last Friday Liam had $65.46. Over the weekend he received some money for cleaning the attic. He now has $60. How much money did he receive?

6) After paying $17.36 for a sandwich, Elise has $31.23. How much money did she have before buying the sandwich?

Two–Step Equations

✎ **Solve each equation.**

1) $6(8 + x) = 18$

2) $(-8)(x - 6) = 72$

3) $(-11)(2x - 3) = (-33)$

4) $8(5 + 2x) = 72$

5) $15(2x - 4) = 120$

6) $2(2x + 3) = 14$

7) $9(11 + 2x) = (-36)$

8) $(-12)(3x + 2) = 60$

9) $6(x + 5) = 30$

10) $\frac{4x - 12}{4} = 8$

11) $(-18) = \frac{x + 16}{3}$

12) $180 = (-3)(8x + 4)$

13) $\frac{x}{5} - 18 = 2$

14) $45 = 15 + \frac{x}{5}$

15) $\frac{-36 + x}{6} = (-16)$

16) $(-5)(10 + 2x) = (-150)$

17) $(-2x) + 24 = 98$

18) $\frac{-6 + 7x}{4} = (-5)$

19) $\frac{x + 5}{5} = (-9)$

20) $(-7) + \frac{x}{3} = (-18)$

Two–Step Equation Word Problems

✎Solve.

1) The sum of 5 consecutive even numbers is 160. What is the smallest of these numbers?

2) How old am I if 900 reduced by 3 times my age is750?

3) For a field trip, 6 students rode in a car and the rest filled seven buses. How many students were in each bus if 517 students were on the trip?

4) The sum of three consecutive numbers is 147. What is the largest of these numbers?

5) You bought a magazine for $10 and seven erasers. You spent a total of $59. How much did each eraser cost?

Multi–Step Equations

✍ **Solve each equation.**

1) $-(3-4x) = 17$

2) $-28 = -(6x+4)$

3) $7x - 20 = (-7x) + 8$

4) $-60 = (-14x) - 16x$

5) $4(1+3x) + 8x = -116$

6) $5x - 10 = 19 + 3x - 4 + x$

7) $10 - 4x = (-14) - x + x$

8) $18 - 17x - 14x = 8 - 9x$

9) $15 + 2x + 8x = (-10) + 5x$

10) $(-6x) - 5(-10 + x) = 226$

11) $18 = (-9x) - 17 + 17$

12) $48 = 5x - 12 + 7x$

13) $9(4 + 5x) = 441$

14) $100 = (-14x) - 6x$

15) $16x - 3 = (-5) + 14x$

16) $26x - 18 = 24x + 16$

17) $140 = (4x - 4)$

18) $(-41) - 2x = 5(2 + 3x)$

19) $10x + 13 = -3(2 + 3x)$

20) $4 = 1 - 7x + 3$

Answers of Worksheets – Chapter 7

One–Step Equations

1) 12	6) -22	11) -21	16) 11
2) 40	7) -13	12) -17	17) 45
3) -21	8) 3	13) -8	18) 10
4) 9	9) 16	14) 12	19) -9
5) -32	10) 5	15) 5	20) 17

One–Step Equation Word Problems

1) 8	3) 18	5) 5.46
2) \$69.68	4) 38	6) 48.59

Two–Step Equations

1) -5	6) 2	11) -70	17) -37
2) -3	7) $-\frac{15}{2}$	12) -8	18) -2
3) 3	8) $-\frac{7}{3}$	13) 100	19) -50
4) 2	9) 0	14) 150	20) -33
5) 6	10) 11	15) -60	
		16) 10	

Two–Step Equation Word Problems

1) 30	3) 73	5) \$7
2) 50	4) 50	

Multi–Step Equations

1) 5	6) 25	11) -2	16) 17
2) 4	7) 6	12) 5	17) 36
3) 2	8) $\frac{5}{11}$	13) 9	18) -3
4) 2	9) -5	14) -5	19) -1
5) -6	10) -16	15) -1	20) 0

Chapter 8: Inequalities

Topics that you'll learn in this chapter:

- ✓ Graphing Single– Variable Inequalities

- ✓ One– Step Inequalities

- ✓ Two– Step Inequalities

- ✓ Multi– Step Inequalities

Graphing Single–Variable Inequalities

✍ **Draw a graph for each inequality.**

1) $5 \geq x$

2) $x < -5$

3) $-4 < x$

4) $-x \geq 2$

5) $x > 0$

6) $-1.5 \leq x$

One–Step Inequalities

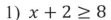 Solve each inequality and graph it.

1) $x + 2 \geq 8$

2) $x - 5 \leq 6$

3) $-6x < 3$

4) $-x + 3 > -10$

5) $x + 7 \geq -9$

6) $5x < 10$

7) $4x > -16$

Two–Step Inequalities

✎ **Solve each inequality.**

1) $6x - 6 \leq 6$

2) $2x - 4 \leq 2$

3) $3x - 5 \leq 10$

4) $5x + 6 \geq 26$

5) $4x - 5 \geq 15$

6) $4x - 4 \leq 8$

7) $2x - 6 \leq 4$

8) $3x + 4 \leq 7$

9) $9x + 23 \leq 23$

10) $11x - 5 \leq 6$

11) $3x - 15 < 15$

12) $2x - 8 < 20$

13) $6 + 4x \geq 14$

14) $10 - 2x < 20$

15) $5 - 8x \geq 13$

16) $9 - 4x \leq 1$

Multi–Step Inequalities

✎ **Solve each inequality.**

1) $\frac{6x}{6} - 1 < 5$

2) $\frac{2x + 5}{3} \leq 5$

3) $\frac{4x - 9}{3} > 1$

4) $-5(x - 7) > 30$

5) $4 + \frac{x}{3} < 7$

6) $\frac{5x + 3}{2} \leq 9$

Answers of Worksheets – Chapter 8

Graphing Single–Variable Inequalities

1) $5 \geq x$

2) $x < -5$

3) $-4 < x$

4) $-x \geq 2$

5) $x > 0$

6) $-1.5 \leq x$

One–Step Inequalities

1)

2)

3)

4)
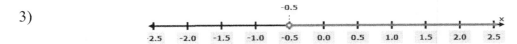

5)

6)
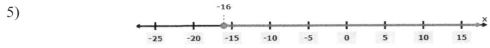

7)

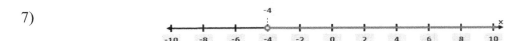

Two–Step inequalities

1) $x \leq 2$

2) $x \leq 3$

3) $x \leq 5$

4) $x \geq 4$

5) $x \geq 5$

6) $x \leq 3$

7) $x \leq 5$

8) $x \leq 1$

9) $x \leq 0$

10) $x \leq 1$

11) $x < 10$

12) $x < 14$

13) $x \geq 2$

14) $x > -5$

15) $x \leq -1$

16) $x \geq 2$

Multi–Step inequalities.

1) $x < 6$

2) $x \leq 5$

3) $x > 3$

4) $x < 1$

5) $x < 9$

6) $x \leq 3$

Chapter 9: Functions

Topics that you'll learn in this chapter:

- ✓ Relations and Functions

- ✓ Finding Slope and Rate of Change

- ✓ Find the x–intercept and y–intercept

- ✓ Graphing Lines Using Slope–Intercept Form

- ✓ Slope-Intercept Form

- ✓ Point-Slope Form

- ✓ Equation of parallel or perpendicular lines

- ✓ Graphing Lines of Equations

- ✓ Equations of horizontal and vertical lines

- ✓ Function Notation

- ✓ Adding and Subtracting Functions

- ✓ Multiplying and Dividing Functions

- ✓ Solving Quadratic Functions

Relation and Functions

✎ **State the domain and range of each relation. Then determine whether each relation is a function.**

1)

Function:

....

Domain:

....

Range:

....

2)

Function:

....

Domain:

....

Range:

....

x	y
3	4
0	1
−2	−3
6	−3
8	2

3)

Function:

....

Domain:

....

Range:

....

4) $\{(1, -2), (4, -1), (0, 5), (4, 0), (3, 8)\}$

Function:

....

Domain:

....

Range:

....

5)

Function:

....

Domain:

....

Range:

....

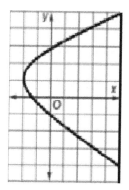

6)

Function:

....

Domain:

....

Range:

....

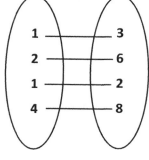

Slope and Rate of Change

✍ **Find the slope of the line through each pair of points.**

1) $(3, 4), (2, 5)$

2) $(2, -5), (-4, 3)$

3) $(2, -9), (5, -6)$

4) $(14, 7), (20, 12)$

5) $(1, -5), (8, -4)$

6) $(13, -9), (15, -7)$

7) $(-5, -8), (-8, -2)$

8) $(0, 0), (12, -2)$

9) $(14, -8), (-6, 5)$

10) $(-2, 5), (-2, 8)$

11) $(-14, -9), (-6, -15)$

12) $(-19, 2), (2, -19)$

✍ **Write the slope–intercept form of the equation of the line through the given points.**

1) Through: $(4, 3), (5, 2)$

2) Through: $(-3, -2), (-7, -4)$

3) Through: $(0.8, 2), (4, 2.8)$

4) Through: $(8, -5), (3, 0)$

5) Through: $(-2, 1), (-3, 4)$

6) Through: $(6, -1), (2, 7)$

7) Through: $(5, 7), (3, 6)$

8) Through: $(-1.5, 2), (6.5, -2)$

9) Through: $(2, -1), (6, 11)$

10) Through: $(4, 1), (-2, 7)$

11) Through: $(2, 4), (-2, -4)$

12) Through: $(4, 5), (0, -1)$

Find the value of b: The line that passes through each pair of points has the given slope.

1) $(5, -4), (2, b), m = 1$

2) $(b, -4), (-4, 1), m = -\frac{1}{3}$

3) $(-4, b), (4, 8), m = \frac{1}{2}$

4) $(0, 3), (b, 8), m = 1\frac{2}{3}$

✎ Write the slope intercept form of the equation of each line

1)

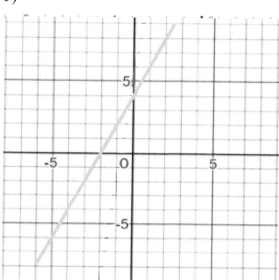

2)

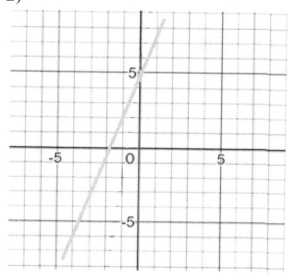

3)

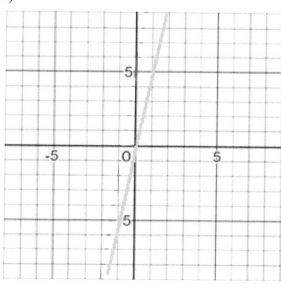

4)

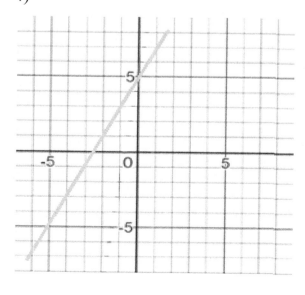

Rate of change

✍ **What is the average rate of change of the function?**

1) $f(x) = 3x^2 + 5$, from $x = 3$ to $x = 6$?

2) $f(x) = -2x^2 - 4$, from $x = 2$ to $x = 4$?

3) $f(x) = x^3 + 3$, from $x = 1$ to $x = 2$?

x and y intercepts

✍ Find the x and y intercepts for the following equations.

1) $5x + 3y = 15$

2) $y = x + 8$

3) $4x = y + 16$

4) $x + y = -2$

5) $4x - 3y = 7$

6) $7y - 5x + 10 = 0$

7) $\frac{3}{7}x + \frac{1}{4}y + \frac{2}{3} = 0$

8) $3x - 21 = 0$

9) $24 - 4y = 0$

10) $-2x - 6y + 42 = 12$

Slope–intercept Form

✎ **Write the slope–intercept form of the equation of each line.**

1) $-14x + y = 6$

2) $-2(7x + y) = 24$

3) $-8x - 16y = -48$

4) $5x + 14 = -3y$

5) $x - 3y = 12$

6) $18x - 12y = -6$

7) $28x - 14y = -56$

8) $7x - 4y + 25 = 0$

9) $-\frac{1}{3}y = -2x + 3$

10) $5 - y - 4x = 0$

11) $-y = -6x - 9$

12) $10x + 5y = -15$

13) $3(x + y + 2) = 0$

14) $y - 4 = x + 3$

15) $3(y + 3) = 2(x - 3)$

16) $\frac{3}{4}y + \frac{1}{4}x + \frac{5}{4} = 0$

Point–slope Form

✍ **Find the slope of the following lines. Name a point on each line.**

1) $y = 2(x + 3)$

2) $y + 4 = \dfrac{1}{3}(x - 1)$

3) $y + 3 = -1.5x$

4) $y - 3 = \dfrac{1}{2}(x - 2)$

5) $y + 2 = 0.4(x + 3)$

6) $y - 8 = -3x$

7) $y - 12 = -3(x - 8)$

8) $y + 14 = 0$

9) $y + 18 = 2(x + 5)$

10) $y - 17 = -8(x - 3)$

✍ **Write an equation in point–slope form for the line that passes through the given point with the slope provided.**

11) $(2, -3), m = 4$

12) $(-7, 4), m = \dfrac{1}{5}$

13) $(0, -6), m = -2$

14) $(-a, b), m = m$

15) $(-9, 1), m = 3$

16) $(3, 0), m = -5$

17) $(-4, 11), m = \dfrac{1}{3}$

18) $(0, 11), m = 0$

19) $\left(-\dfrac{1}{3}, 3\right), m = \dfrac{1}{5}$

20) $(0, 0), m = -3$

Equation of Parallel or Perpendicular Lines

✎ Write an equation of the line that passes through the given point and is

parallel to the given line.

1) $(-1, -2), x + 3y = -11$

2) $(-4, 1), y = x - 5$

3) $(-2, 0), 2y = 5x - 3$

4) $(0, 0), -3y + 4x - 14 = 0$

5) $(1, 10), y + 15 = 0$

6) $(0, 7), -5x - y = -4$

7) $(-2, -1), y = \frac{4}{5}x + 3$

8) $(-2, 5), -8x + 5y = -18$

9) $(3, -2), y = -\frac{2}{5}x - 3$

10) $(-5, -5), 6x + 15y = -30$

✎ Write an equation of the line that passes through the given point and is

perpendicular to the given line.

11) $(-2, -6), 3x + 4y = -8$

12) $(-\frac{1}{3}, \frac{3}{5}), 4x - 8y = -32$

13) $(2, -5), y = -5$

14) $(7, -2), x = 7$

15) $(0, -3), y = \frac{1}{2}x + 6$

16) $(\frac{3}{5}, \frac{2}{5}), y = -6x - 24$

17) $(-10, 0), y = \frac{5}{3}x - 15$

18) $(3, -5), y = x + 12$

19) $(-3, -1), y = \frac{7}{3}x - 4$

20) $(0, 0), y - 8x + 6 = 0$

Graphing Lines of Equations

✎ **Sketch the graph of each line**

1) $y = 4x - 3$

2) $y = -\frac{1}{3}x + \frac{3}{4}$

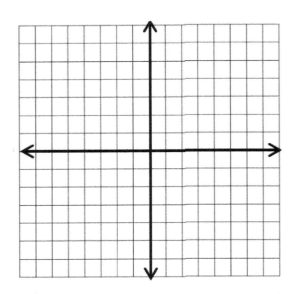
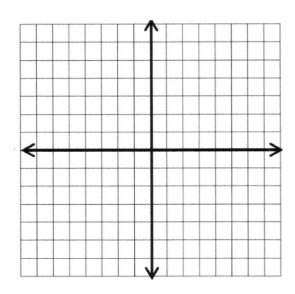

3) $5x - 3y = 10$

4) $-2x - y = 4$

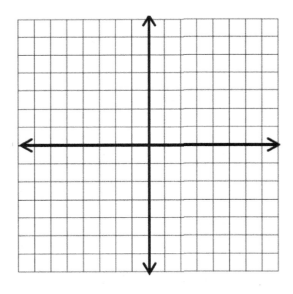
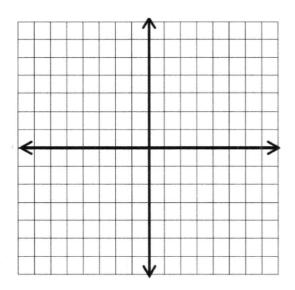

Equations of Horizontal and Vertical Lines

✎Sketch the graph of each line.

1) $y = 3$

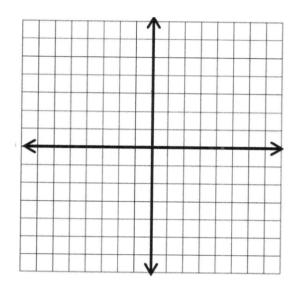

2) $y = -1$

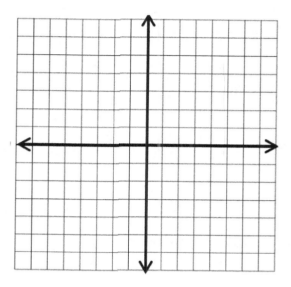

3) $x = 0$

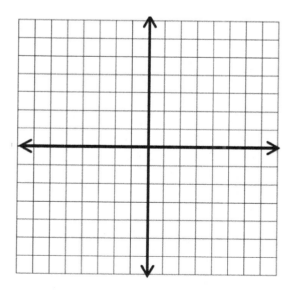

4) $x = 3$

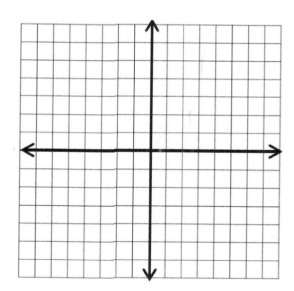

Answers of Worksheets – Chapter 9

Relation and Functions

1) No, $D_f = \{1, 3, 5, 7, 9\}$, $R_f = \{3, 5, 8, 12, 18\}$

2) Yes, $D_f = \{3, 0, -2, 6, 8\}$, $R_f = \{4, 1, -3, \ 2\}$

3) Yes, $D_f = (-\infty, \infty)$, $R_f = \{2, -\infty)$

4) No, $D_f = \{1, 4, 0, 3\}$, $R_f = \{-2, -1, 5, 0, 8\}$

5) No, $D_f = [-2, \infty)$, $R_f = (-\infty, \infty)$

6) No, $D_f = \{1, 2, 4\}$, $R_f = \{3, 6, 2, 8\}$

Finding Slope

1) -1

2) $-\dfrac{4}{3}$

3) 1

4) $\dfrac{5}{6}$

5) $\dfrac{1}{7}$

6) 1

7) -2

8) $-\dfrac{1}{6}$

9) $-\dfrac{13}{20}$

10) Undefined

11) $-\dfrac{3}{4}$

12) -1

Writing Linear Equations

1) $y = -x + 7$

2) $y = 0.5x + -0.5$

3) $y = \dfrac{1}{4}x + \dfrac{9}{5}$

4) $y = -x + 3$

5) $y = -3x - 5$

6) $y = -2x + 11$

7) $y = \dfrac{1}{2}x + \dfrac{9}{2}$

8) $y = -0.5x + 1.25$

9) $y = 3x - 7$

10) $y = -x + 5$

11) $y = 2x$

12) $y = 1.5x - 1$

Find the value of b

1) -7

2) 11

3) 4

4) 3

Write an equation from a graph

1) $y = 2x + 4$

2) $y = 3x + 5$

3) $y = 5x$

4) $y = 2x + 5$

Rate of change

1) 27

2) -12

3) 7

x–intercept and y–intercept

1) $y - intercept = 5$ $x - intercept = 3$

2) $y - intercept = 8$ $x - intercept = -8$

3) $y - intercept = -16$ $x - intercept = 4$

4) $y - intercept = -2$ $x - intercept = -2$

5) $y - intercept = -\frac{7}{3}$ $x - intercept = \frac{7}{4}$

6) $y - intercept = -\frac{10}{7}$ $x - intercept = 2$

7) $y - intercept = -\frac{8}{3}$ $x - intercept = -\frac{2}{7}$

8) $y - intercept = undefind$ $x - intercept = 7$

9) $y - intercept = 6$ $x - intercept = undefind$

10) $y - intercept = 5$ $x - intercept = 15$

Slope–intercept form

1) $y = 14x + 6$

2) $y = -7x - 12$

3) $y = -\frac{1}{2}x + 3$

4) $y = -\frac{5}{3}x - \frac{14}{3}$

5) $y = \frac{x}{3} - 4$

6) $y = \frac{3}{2}x + \frac{1}{2}$

7) $y = 2x + 4$

8) $y = \frac{7}{4}x + \frac{25}{4}$

9) $y = 6x - 9$

10) $y = -4x + 5$

11) $y = 6x + 9$

12) $y = -2x - 3$

13) $y = -x - 2$

14) $y = x + 7$

15) $y = \frac{2}{3}x - 5$

16) $y = -\frac{1}{3}x - \frac{5}{3}$

Point–slope form

1) $m = 2, (-3, 0)$

2) $m = \frac{1}{3}, (1, -4)$

3) $m = -\frac{3}{2}, (0, -3)$

4) $m = \frac{1}{2}, (2, 3)$

5) $m = \frac{4}{10}, (-3, -2)$

6) $m = -3, (0, 8)$

7) $m = -3, (8, 12)$

8) $m = 0, (0, -14)$

9) $m = 2, (-5, -18)$

10) $m = -8, (-3, 17)$

11) $y + 3 = 4(x - 2)$

12) $y - 4 = \frac{1}{5}(x + 7)$

13) $y + 6 = -2x$

14) $y - b = m(x + a)$

15) $y - 1 = 3(x + 9)$

16) $y = -5(x - 3)$

17) $y - 11 = \frac{1}{3}(x + 4)$

18) $y - 11 = 0$

19) $y - 3 = \frac{1}{5}\left(x + \frac{1}{3}\right)$

20) $y = -3x$

Equation of parallel or perpendicular line.

1) $y = -\frac{1}{3}x - 2\frac{1}{3}$

2) $y = x + 5$

3) $y = \frac{5}{2}x + 5$

4) $y = \frac{4}{3}x$

5) $y = 10$

6) $y = -5x + 7$

7) $y = \frac{4}{5}x + \frac{3}{5}$

8) $y = \frac{8}{5}x + \frac{41}{5}$

9) $y = -\frac{2}{5}x - \frac{4}{5}$

10) $y = -\frac{2}{5}x - 7$

11) $y = \frac{4}{3}x - \frac{10}{3}$

12) $y = -2x - \frac{1}{15}$

13) $x = 2$

14) $y = -2$

15) $y = -2x - 3$

16) $y = \frac{1}{6}x + \frac{3}{10}$

17) $y = -\frac{3}{5}x - 6$

18) $y = -x - 2$

19) $y = -\frac{3}{7}x - \frac{16}{7}$

20) $y = -\frac{1}{8}x$

1) $y = 4x - 3$

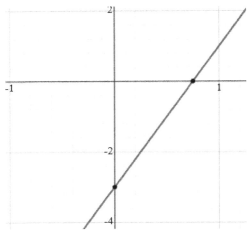

5) $y = -\frac{1}{3}x + \frac{3}{4}$

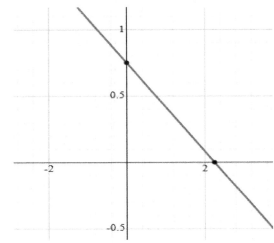

3) $5x - 3y = 10$

4) $-2x - y = 4$

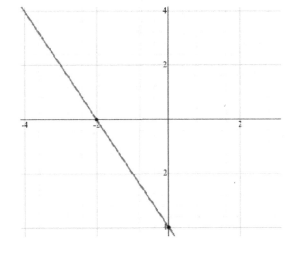

Equations of horizontal and vertical lines

1) $y = 3$

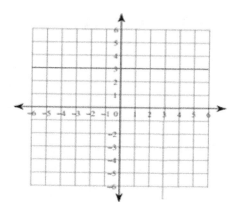

2) $y = -1$(it is on x axes)

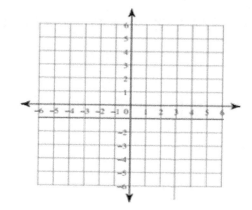

3) $x = 0$

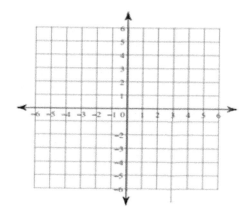

4) $x = 3$

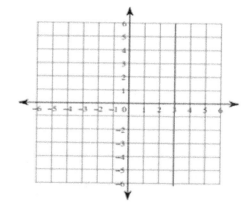

Chapter 10: Transformations

Topics that you'll learn in this chapter:

- ✓ Translations
- ✓ Reflections
- ✓ Rotations
- ✓ Dilations
- ✓ Coordinate of Vertices

Translations

✍ **Graph the image of the figure using the transformation given.**

1) translation: 2 units right and 1 units down

2) translation: 4 units left and 2 units down

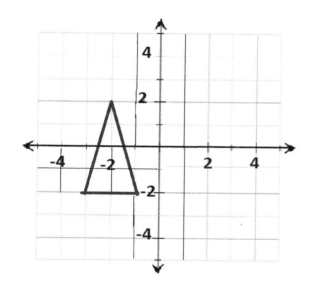

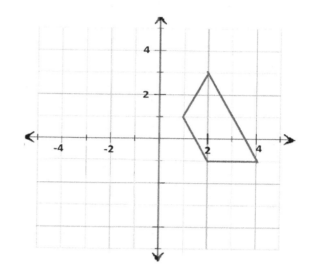

✍ **Write a rule to describe each transformation.**

3)

4)

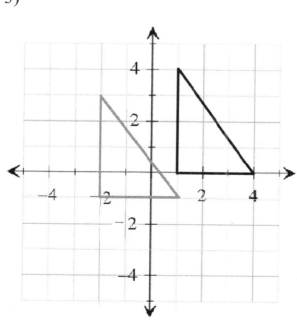

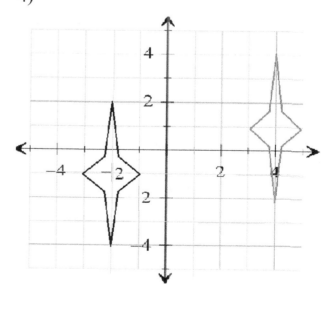

Reflections

✍ **Graph the image of the figure using the transformation given.**

1) Reflection across x = −1

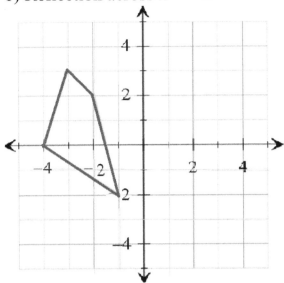

2) Reflection across y = x

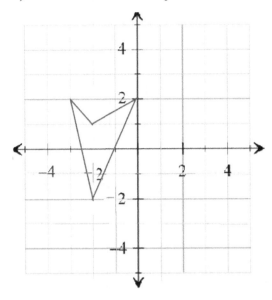

✍ **Write a rule to describe each transformation.**

3)

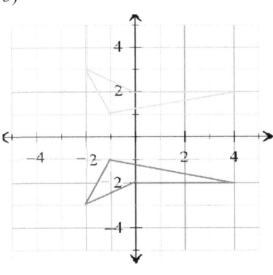

4)

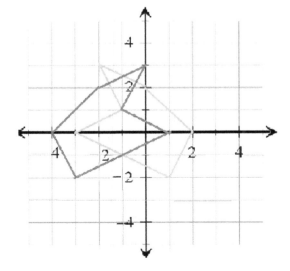

Rotations

✎**Graph the image of the figure using the transformation given.**

1) rotation 270° clockwise about the origin   2) rotation 90° about the origin

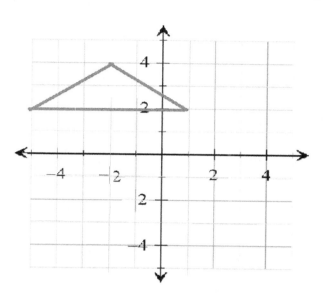
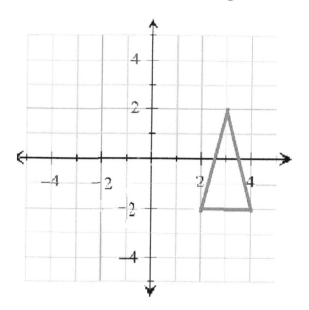

✎**Write a rule to describe each transformation.**

3)   4)

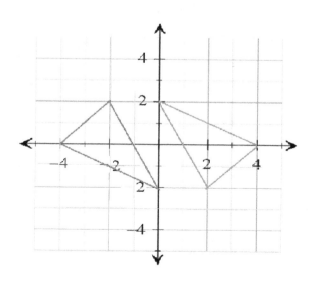
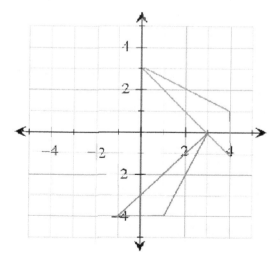

Dilations

✍ **Draw a dilation of the figure using the given scale factor.**

1) $k = \frac{1}{2}$

2) $k = 3$

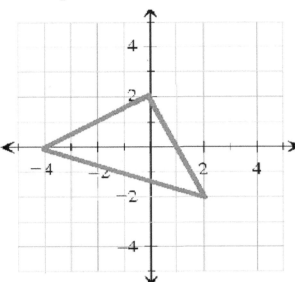

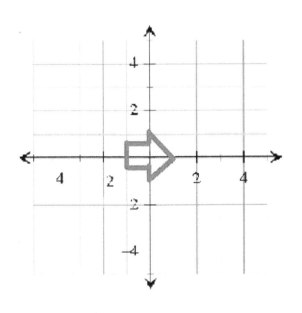

✍ **Determine whether the dilation from figure M to figure N is a reduction or an enlargement. Then find the scale factor and the missing length.**

3)

4)

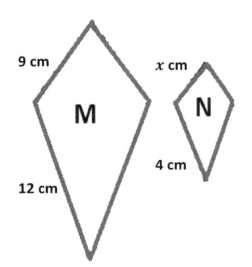

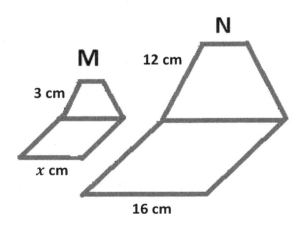

Coordinates of Vertices

✎Calculate the new coordinates after the given transformations.

1) Translate: 3 units right and 2 units down.

   $A(-2,0), B(-3,-4), C(1,5)$

2) Rotation: 90° clockwise about the origin.

   $D(-1,1), E(-3,5), F(-4,2), G(-2,6)$

3) Rotation: 180° about the origin.

   $P(3,2), Q(2,3), R(4,4), S(1,-3)$

4) Rotation: 270° clockwise.

   $J(-5,2), K(-8,4), L(0,3)$

5) Reflection: over the y axis.

   $C(-2,3), D(-6,1), W(1,2), Y(7,-4)$

6) Reflection: across the line $y = x$.

   $A(3,-2), B(5,-4), C(4,-6), D(2,-5)$

7) Reflection: across the line $y = -5$.

   $K(-3,-2), L(-4,-1), M(-1,-4), N(-6,-3)$

8) Dilate: Reduction by scale factor $\frac{1}{2}$.

   $A(4,5), B(-6,-3), C(-3,8)$

9) Dilate: Enlargement by scale factor 2.

   $F(-1,1), G(-4,0), H(3,5)$

Answers of Worksheets – Chapter 10

Translations

1)

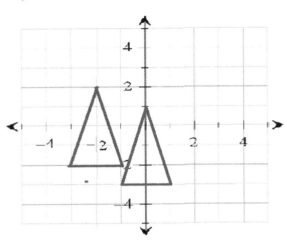

2)

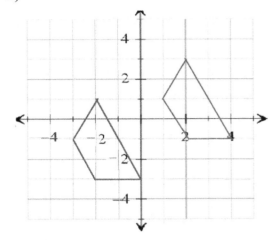

3) translation: : 3 units left and 1 units down

4) translation: 6 units right and 2 unit up

Reflections

1)

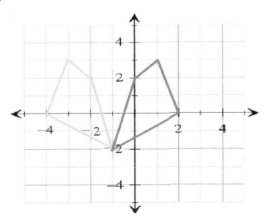

2)

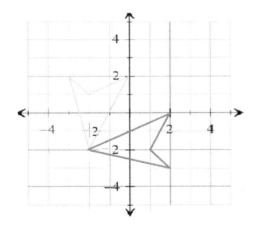

3) reflection across the x-axis

4) reflection across x = -1

Rotations

1) rotation 270° clockwise about the origin

2) rotation 90° about the origin

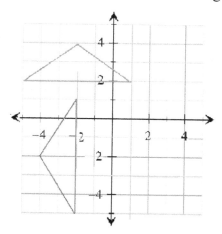

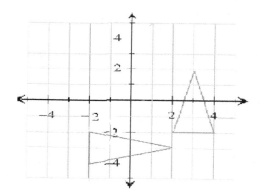

3) rotation 180° about the origin

4) rotation 90° about the origin

Dilations

1)

2)

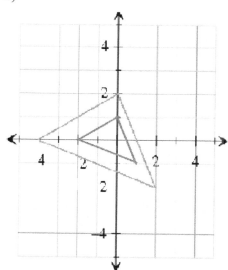

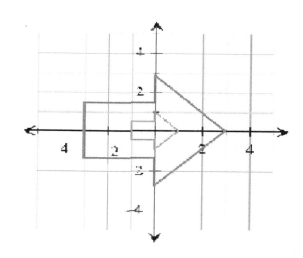

3) Reduction, $k = \frac{1}{3}$, $x = 3\ cm$

4) Enlargement, $k = 4$, $x = 4\ cm$

Coordinate of Vertices

1) $A'(1, -2), B'(0, -6), C'(4,3)$

2) $D'(1,1), E'(5,3), F'(2,4), G'(6,2)$

3) $P'(-3, -2), Q'(-2, -3), R'(-4, -4), S'(-1,3)$

4) $J'(-2, -5), K'(-4, -8), L'(-3,0)$

5) $C'(2,3), D'(6,1), W'(-1,2), Y'(-7,-4)$

6) $A'(-2,3), B'(-4,5), C'(-6,4), D'(-5,2)$

7) $K'(-3,-8), L'(-4,-9), M'(-1,-6), N'(-6,-7)$

8) $A'(2,2.5), B'(-3,-1.5), C'(-1.5,4)$

9) $F'(-2,2), G'(-8,0), H'(6,10)$

Chapter 11: Geometry

Topics that you'll learn in this chapter:

- ➤ The Pythagorean Theorem

- ➤ Area of Triangles and Trapezoids

- ➤ Area and Circumference of Circles

- ➤ Area and Perimeter of Polygons

- ➤ Area of Squares, Rectangles, and Parallelograms

- ➤ Volume of Cubes, Rectangle Prisms, and Cylinder

- ➤ Surface Area of Cubes, Rectangle Prisms, and Cylinder

The Pythagorean Theorem

✍ Do the following lengths form a right triangle?

1)

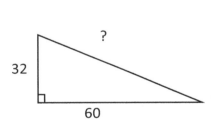

2)

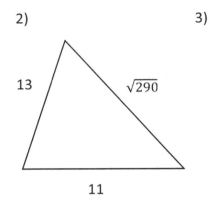

3)

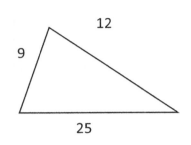

✍ Find each missing length to the nearest tenth.

4)

5)

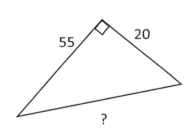

6)

Angles

✍ **What is the value of** x **in the following figures?**

1)
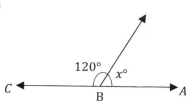

2)
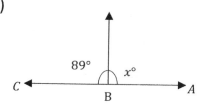

3)
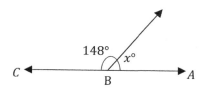

4)
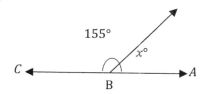

5)
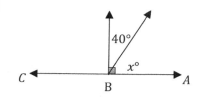

6)
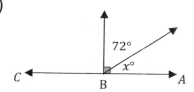

✍ *Solve.*

7) Six supplement peer to each other angles have equal measures. What is the measure of each angle? _____

8) The measure of an angle is one fourth the measure of its complementary. What is the measure of the angle? _____

Area of Triangles

Find the area of each.

1)

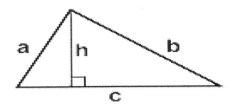

c = 15 mi

h = 4 mi

2)

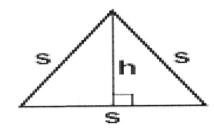

s = 6 m

h = 5.2 m

3)

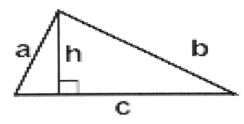

a = 9.5 m

b = 25 m

c = 18 m

h = 9 m

4)

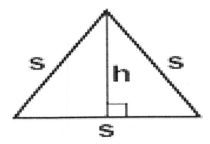

s = 8 m

h = 6.93 m

Area of Trapezoids

✎ Calculate the area for each trapezoid.

1)

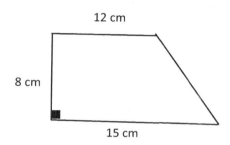

12 cm

8 cm

15 cm

2)

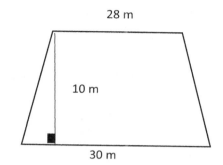

28 m

10 m

30 m

3)

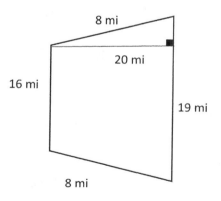

8 mi

20 mi

16 mi

19 mi

8 mi

4)

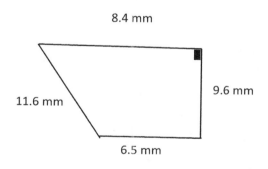

8.4 mm

11.6 mm

9.6 mm

6.5 mm

Area and Perimeter of Polygons

✏️**Find the area and perimeter of each**

1)

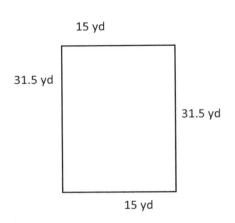

15 yd

31.5 yd

31.5 yd

15 yd

2)

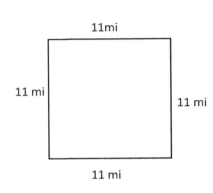

11mi

11 mi

11 mi

11 mi

3)

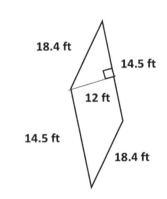

18.4 ft

14.5 ft

12 ft

14.5 ft

18.4 ft

4)

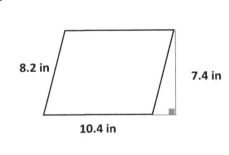

8.2 in

7.4 in

10.4 in

5)

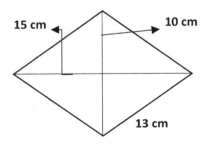

15 cm

10 cm

13 cm

6)

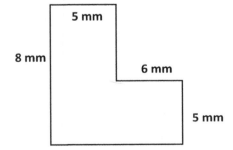

5 mm

8 mm

6 mm

5 mm

✏️**Find the perimeter of each shape.**

7)

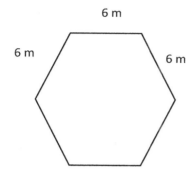

6 m

6 m

6 m

8)

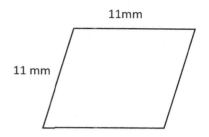

11mm

11 mm

9)

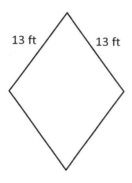

13 ft

13 ft

10)

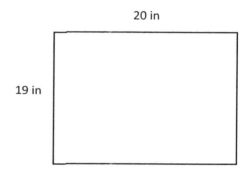

20 in

19 in

11)

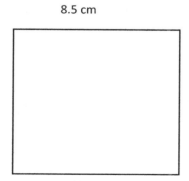

8.5 cm

12)

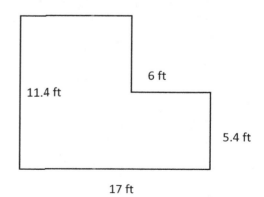

6 ft

11.4 ft

5.4 ft

17 ft

Area and Circumference of Circles

✎ **Find the area and circumference of each.** ($\pi = 3.14$)

1)

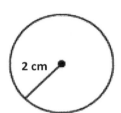

2 cm

2)

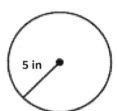

5 in

3)

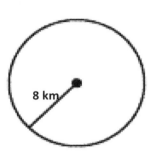

8 km

4)

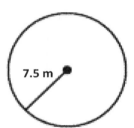

7.5 m

5)

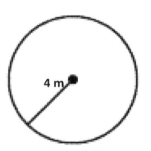

4 m

6)

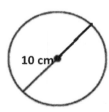

10 cm

7)

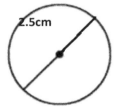

2.5cm

8)

1.5 in

Volume of Cubes

✍ Find the volume of each.

1)

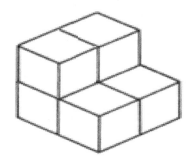

2)

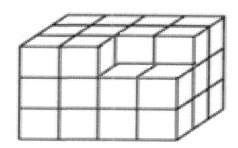

3)

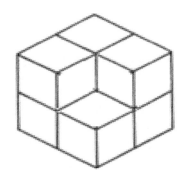

4)

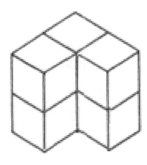

5)

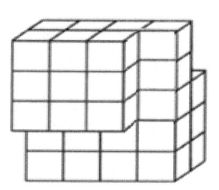

6)

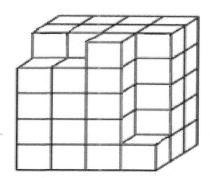

Volume of Rectangle Prisms

✎Find the volume of each of the rectangular prisms.

1)

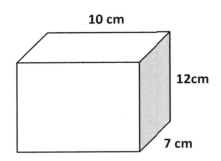

10 cm
12cm
7 cm

2)

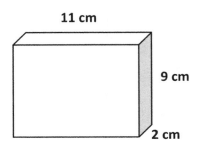

11 cm
9 cm
2 cm

3)

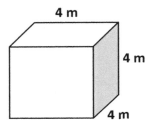

4 m
4 m
4 m

4)

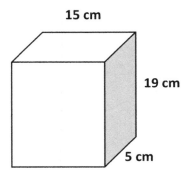

15 cm
19 cm
5 cm

5)

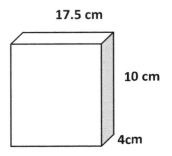

17.5 cm
10 cm
4cm

6)

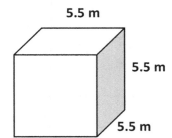

5.5 m
5.5 m
5.5 m

Surface Area of Cubes

✎ Find the surface of each cube.

1)

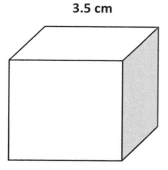

7 mm

2)

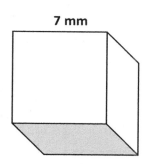

10.5 mm

3)

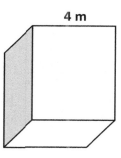

3.5 cm

4)

4 m

5)

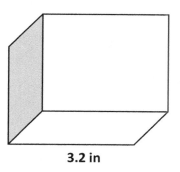

3.2 in

6)

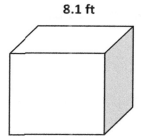

8.1 ft

Surface Area of a Rectangle Prism

✍ **Find the surface of each prism.**

1)

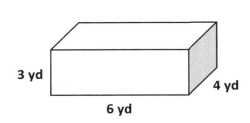

3 yd

4 yd

6 yd

2)

1.02 mm

1.5 mm

0.5 mm

3)

2.5 in

9.5 in

4 in

4)

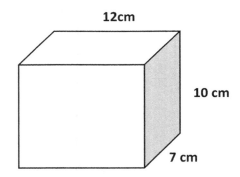

12cm

10 cm

7 cm

Volume of a Cylinder

✎ **Find the volume of each cylinder.** ($\pi = 3.14$)

1)

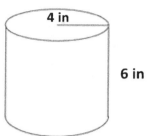

4 in

6 in

2)

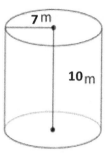

7 m

10 m

3)

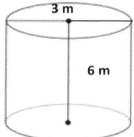

3 m

6 m

4)

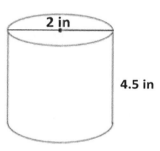

2 in

4.5 in

5)

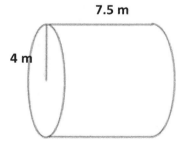

7.5 m

4 m

6)

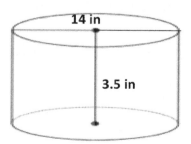

14 in

3.5 in

Surface Area of a Cylinder

✏ **Find the surface of each cylinder.** ($\pi = 3.14$)

1)

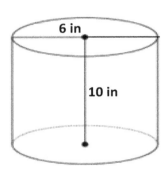

5 ft

8 ft

2)

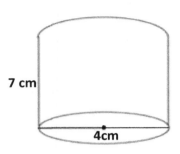

7 cm

4cm

3)

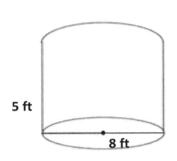

6 in

10 in

4)

2 yd

5.5 yd

5)

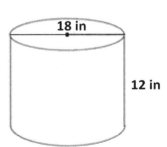

18 in

12 in

6)

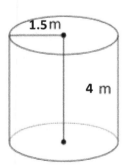

1.5 m

4 m

Answers of Worksheets – Chapter 11

The Pythagorean Theorem

1) yes

2) yes

3) no

4) 68

5) 62.92

6) 58.52

Angles

1) 60°

2) 91°

3) 32°

4) 25°

5) 50°

6) 18°

7) 30°

8) 18°

Area of Triangles

1) 30 mi²

2) 15.6 m²

3) 81 m²

4) 27.72m²

Area of Trapezoids

1) 108 cm²

2) 290 m²

3) 350 mi²

4) 71.52 mm²

Area of Squares, Rectangles, and Parallelograms

1) Area: 472.5 m^2, Perimeter: 93m

2) Area: 121 mm^2, Perimeter: 44mm

3) Area: 174 ft^2, Perimeter: 65.8 ft

4) Area: 76.96 in^2, Perimeter: 37.2in

5) Area: 75cm^2, Perimeter 52 cm

6) Area: 70 mm^2, Perimeter:38 mm

7) P: 36 m

8) P: 44 mm

9) P: 52 ft

10) P: 78 in

11) P: 34 cm

12) P: 56.8 ft

Area and Circumference of Circles

1) Area: 12.56 cm², Circumference: 12.56 cm.

2) Area: 78.5 in², Circumference: 31.4 in.

3) Area: 200.96 km², Circumference: 50.24 km.

4) Area: 176.625 m², Circumference: 47.1 m.

5) Area: 50.24 m^2, Circumference: 25.12 m

6) Area: 78.5 cm^2, Circumference: 31.4 cm.

7) Area: 4.906 cm^2, Circumference: 7.85 cm.

8) Area: 1.766 in^2, Circumference: 4.71 in.

Volumes of Cubes

1) 6   3) 7   5) 41

2) 34   4) 6   6) 54

Volume of Rectangle Prisms

1) 840 cm^3 3) 64 m^3 5) 700 cm^3

2) 198 cm^3 4) 1,425 cm^3 6) 166.375 cm^3

Surface Area of a Cube

1) 294 mm^2 4) 96 m^2

2) 661.5 mm^2 5) 61.44 in^2

3) 73.5 cm^2 6) 393.66 ft^2

Surface Area of a Rectangle Prism

1) 108 yd^2 3) 143.5 in^2

2) 5.58 mm^2 4) 548 cm^2

Volume of a Cylinder

1) 301.44 cm^3 3) 42.39 m^3 5) 376.8 m^3

2) 1538.6cm^3 4) 14.13 m^3 6) 538.51 m^3

Surface Area of a Cylinder

1) 226.08 ft^2 3) 224.92 in^2 5) 1,186.92 in^2

2) 113.04 cm^2 4) 94.2 yd^2 6) 51.81m^2

Chapter 12: Statistics

Topics that you'll learn in this chapter:

- ➢ Mean, Median, Mode, and Range of the Given Data

- ➢ Box and Whisker Plots

- ➢ Bar Graph

- ➢ Stem– And– Leaf Plot

- ➢ The Pie Graph or Circle Graph

- ➢ Dot and Scatter Plots

- ➢ Probability of Simple Events

Mean and Median

✎Find Mean and Median of the Given Data.

1) 8, 10, 7, 3, 12

2) 4, 6, 9, 7, 5, 19

3) 5, 11, 1, 1, 8, 9 , 20

4) 12, 4, 2, 7, 3, 2

5) 3, 5, 7, 4, 7, 8, 9

6) 5, 10, 4, 4, 9, 12, 9

7) 10, 4, 8, 5, 9, 6, 7, 19

8) 16, 3, 4, 3, 7, 6, 18

9) 22, 20, 5, 11, 32, 44, 71

10) 14, 8, 9, 5, 4, 13, 8, 10

11) 8, 15, 35, 66, 41, 21

12) 24, 23, 54, 38, 71, 81

✎ Solve.

13) In a javelin throw competition, five athletics score 23, 45, 53.53, 13 and 61 meters. What are their Mean and Median? _____

14) Eva went to shop and bought 7 apples, 4 peaches, 6 bananas, 3 pineapple and 4 melons. What are the Mean and Median of her purchase? _____

Mode and Range

✎ **Find Mode and Rage of the Given Data.**

1) 10, 12, 8, 8,4, 1, 9

   Mode: _____ Range: _____

2) 4, 6, 4, 13, 2, 13, 19, 13

   Mode: _____ Range: _____

3) 8, 8, 7, 2, 7, 7, 5, 6, 5

   Mode: _____ Range: _____

4) 12, 9, 12,6, 12, 9, 10

   Mode: _____ Range: _____

5) 2, 2, 4, 3, 2, 10, 8

   Mode: _____ Range: _____

6) 6, 1, 4, 20, 19, 2, 7, 1, 5, 1

   Mode: _____ Range: _____

7) 16,35, 9, 7, 7, 5, 14, 13, 7

   Mode: _____ Range: _____

8) 7, 6, 6, 9, 16, 6, 7, 5

   Mode: _____ Range: _____

9) 12, 5, 6, 12, 4, 4, 6, 4, 5

   Mode: _____ Range: _____

10) 2, 5, 10, 5, 4, 5, 10, 10

   Mode: _____ Range: _____

11) 4,11, 5, 3, 12, 12, 18, 2

   Mode: _____ Range: _____

12) 6, 3, 3, 9, 6, 16, 3, 10

   Mode: _____ Range: _____

✎**Solve.**

13) A stationery sold 15 pencils, 26 red pens, 22 blue pens, 10 notebooks, 12 erasers, 22 rulers and 42 color pencils. What are the Mode and Range for the stationery sells?

   Mode: _____   Range: _____

14) In an English test, eight students score 24, 13, 17, 21, 19, 13, 13 and 17. What are their Mode and Range? _____

Times Series

✍ **Use the following Graph to complete the table.**

Day	Distance (km)
1	
2	

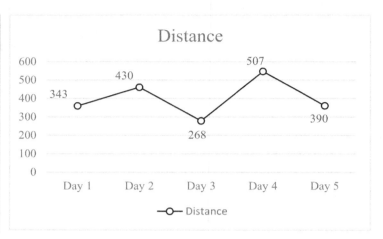

The following table shows the number of births in the US from 2007 to 2012 (in millions).

Year	Number of births (in millions)
2007	6.42
2008	6.45
2009	6.33
2010	5.9
2011	4.35
2012	4.35

Draw a time series for the table.

Box and Whisker Plot

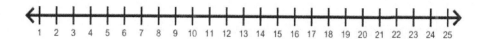Make box and whisker plots for the given data.

$1, 5, 20, 8, 3, 10, 13, 11, 14, 17, 18, 15, 23$

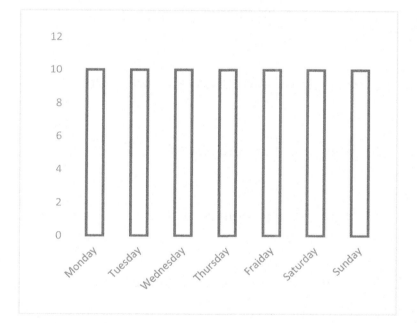

Bar Graph

Graph the given information as a bar graph.

Day	Sale House
Monday	6
Tuesday	4
Wednesday	10
Thursday	5
Friday	2
Saturday	8
Sunday	1

Dot plots

✍ A survey of "How many pets each person owned?" has these results:

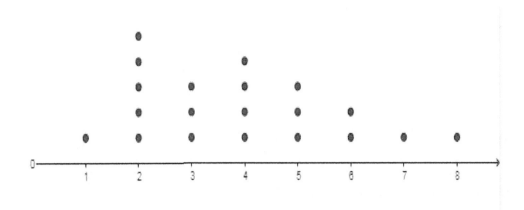

1) How many people have at least 3 pets?

2) How many people have 2 and 3 pets?

3) How many people have 4 pets?

4) How many people have 2 or less than 2 pets?

5) How many people have more than 7 pets?

Scatter Plots

Construct a scatter plot.

x	1	2.5	3	3.5	4	5
y	4	3.5	4.5	2.5	8	2

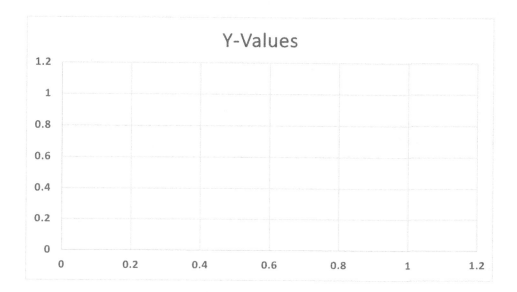

Stem–And–Leaf Plot

✎ Make stem ad leaf plots for the given data.

1) 42, 14, 17, 21, 44, 24, 18, 47, 23, 24, 19, 12

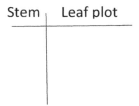

2) 10, 65, 14, 18, 69, 11, 33, 61, 66, 38, 15, 35

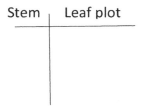

3) 122, 87, 99, 86, 100, 126, 92, 129, 88, 121, 91, 107

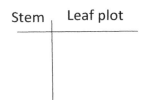

4) 60, 51, 119, 69, 72, 59, 110, 65, 77, 59, 65, 112, 71

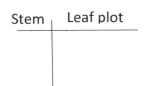

The Pie Graph or Circle Graph

Favorite Sports:

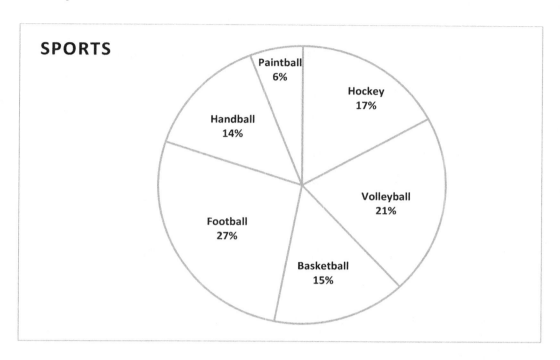

1) What percentage of pie graph is paintball?

2) What percentage of pie graph is Hockey and volleyball?

3) What percentage of pie not Football and Basketball

4) What percentage of pie graph is Hockey and Handball and Football?

5) What percentage of pie graph is Basketball?

6) What percentage of pie not Handball and Paintball?

Probability of Simple Events

✎ **Solve.**

1) A number is chosen at random from 28 to 35. Find the probability of selecting factors of 5.

2) A number is chosen at random from 1 to 60. Find the probability of selecting multiples of 15.

3) Find the probability of selecting 4queens from a deck of card.

4) A number is chosen at random from 8 to 19. Find the probability of selecting factors of 3.

5) What probability of selecting a ball less than 6 from 10 different bingo balls?

6) A number is chosen at random from 1 to 10. What is the probability of selecting a multiple of 2?

7) A card is chosen from a well-shuffled deck of 52 cards. What is the probability that the card will be a king OR a queen?

8) A number is chosen at random from 1 to 20. What is the probability of selecting multiples of 5.

Answers of Worksheets – Chapter 12

Mean and Median

1) Mean: 8, Median: 8

2) Mean: 8.33, Median: 6.5

3) Mean: 7.85, Median: 8

4) Mean: 5, Median: 3.5

5) Mean: 6.14, Median: 7

6) Mean: 7.57, Median: 9

7) Mean: 8.5, Median: 7.5

8) Mean: 8.14, Median: 6

9) Mean: 29.28, Median: 22

10) Mean: 8.87, Median: 8.5

11) Mean: 31, Median: 28

12) Mean: 48.5, Median: 46

13) Mean: 39.106, Median: 45

14) Mean: 4.8, Median: 4

Mode and Range

1) Mode: 8, Range: 11

2) Mode: 13, Range: 17

3) Mode: 7, Range: 6

4) Mode: 12, Range: 6

5) Mode: 2, Range: 8

6) Mode: 1, Range: 19

7) Mode: 7, Range: 30

8) Mode: 6, Range: 11

9) Mode: 4, Range: 8

10) Mode: 5,10, Range: 8

11) Mode: 12, Range: 16

12) Mode: 3, Range: 13

13) Mode: 22, Range: 32

14) Mode: 13, Range: 11

Times Series

Day	Distance (km)
1	343
2	430
3	268
4	507
5	390

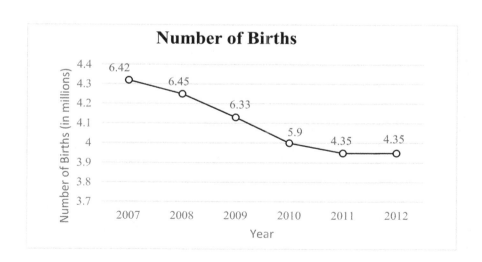

Box and Whisker Plots

1, 3, 5, 8, 10, 11, 13, 14, 15, 17, 18, 20, 23

Maximum: 23, Minimum: 2, Q_1: 8, Q_2: 13, Q_3: 17

Bar Graph

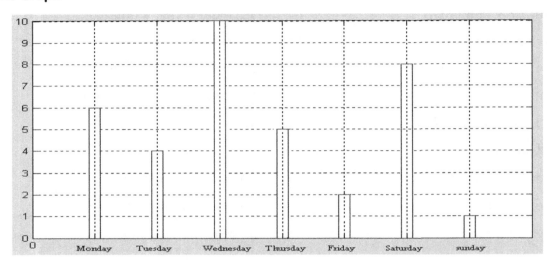

Dot plots

1) 4   3) 4   5) 1

2) 8   4) 6

Scatter Plots

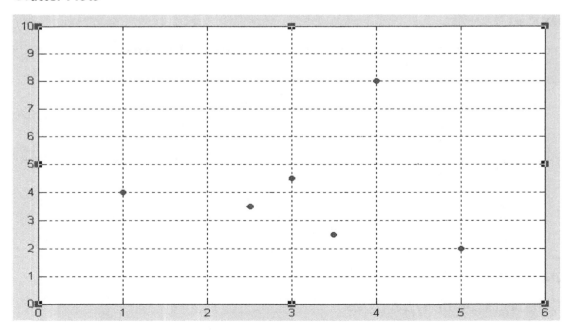

Stem–And–Leaf Plot

1)

Stem	leaf
1	2 4 7 8 9
2	1 3 4
4	2 4 7

2)

Stem	leaf
1	0 1 4 5 8
3	3 5 8
6	1 5 6 9

3)

Stem	leaf
8	6 7 8
9	1 2 9
10	0 7
12	1 2 6 9

4)

Stem	leaf
5	1 9 9
6	0 5 5 9
7	1 2 7
11	0 2 9

The Pie Graph or Circle Graph

1) 6%

2) 38%

3) 58%

4) 58%

5) 15%

6) 80%

Probability of simple events

1) $\frac{1}{4}$

2) $\frac{1}{15}$

3) $\frac{1}{13}$

4) $\frac{1}{3}$

5) $\frac{1}{2}$

6) $\frac{1}{2}$

7) $\frac{2}{13}$

8) $\frac{1}{5}$

9) $\frac{1}{13}$

PSSA Math Practice Tests

Time to Test

Time to refine your skill with a practice examination

Take two practice Grade 7 PSSA Math Tests to simulate the test day experience. After you've finished, score your test using the answer key.

Before You Start

- You'll need a pencil and scratch papers to take the test.
- For this practice test, don't time yourself. Spend time as much as you need.
- It's okay to guess. You won't lose any points if you're wrong.
- After you've finished the test, review the answer key to see where you went go.

Calculators are permitted for students taking the PSSA Mathematics Grade 7

Good Luck!

Grade 7 PSSA Mathematics Formula Sheet

Formulas that you may need to work questions on this test are found below. You may refer to this page at any time during the mathematics test.

Triangle

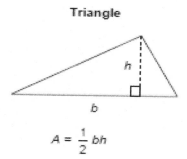

$$A = \frac{1}{2}bh$$

Trapezoid

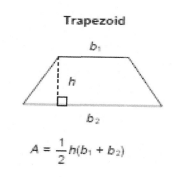

$$A = \frac{1}{2}h(b_1 + b_2)$$

Rectangle

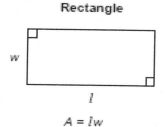

$$A = lw$$

Rectangular Prism

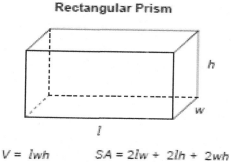

$$V = lwh \qquad SA = 2lw + 2lh + 2wh$$

Square

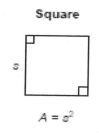

$$A = s^2$$

Cube

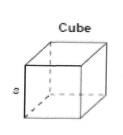

$$V = s \cdot s \cdot s \qquad SA = 6s^2$$

Parallelogram

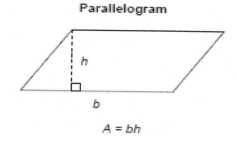

$$A = bh$$

Triangular Prism

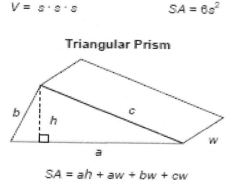

$$SA = ah + aw + bw + cw$$

The Pennsylvania System of School Assessment

Practice Test 1

Mathematics

GRADE 7

❖ **20 Questions**

❖ **Calculators are permitted for this practice test**

Pennsylvania Department of Education Bureau of Curriculum, Assessment and Instruction— *Month Year*

1) The price of a car was $10,000 in 2014, $6,000 in 2015 and $3,600 in 2016.

   What is the rate of depreciation of the price of car per year?

   A. 25 %

   B. 30 %

   C. 40 %

   D. 35 %

2) What is the value of x in the following equation?

$$\frac{3}{7}x + \frac{1}{6} = \frac{1}{3}$$

   A. 15

   B. $\frac{7}{18}$

   C. $\frac{1}{18}$

   D. $\frac{1}{3}$

3) What is the surface area of the cylinder below?

   A. 64 π

   B. 12 π

   C. 68 π

   D. 128 π

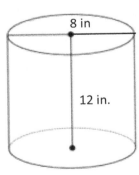

8 in

12 in.

4) Anita's trick–or–treat bag contains 11 pieces of chocolate, 15 suckers, 12 pieces of gum, 12 pieces of licorice. If she randomly pulls a piece of candy from her bag, what is the probability of her pulling out a piece of sucker?

A. $\frac{2}{3}$

B. $\frac{3}{4}$

C. $\frac{5}{6}$

D. $\frac{3}{10}$

5) Which of the following shows the numbers in descending order?

$$0.65, \frac{3}{5}, 97\%, \frac{11}{9}$$

A. $97\%, 0.65, \frac{11}{9}, \frac{3}{5}$

B. $97\%, 0.65, \frac{3}{5}, \frac{11}{9}$

C. $0.65, 97\%, \frac{11}{9}, \frac{3}{5}$

D. $\frac{11}{9}, 97\%, 0.65, \frac{3}{5}$

6) Which of the following points lies on the line $8x + 4y = 12$?

A. $(2, 0)$

B. $(-1, 3)$

C. $(-1, 5)$

D. $(2, 5)$

7) The mean of 35 test scores was calculated as 70. But it turned out that one of the scores was misread as 87 but it was 78. What is the correct mean of the data?

   A. 65.25

   B. 78.75

   C. 69.74

   D. 69.52

8) The width of a box is one third of its length. The height of the box is one third of its width. If the length of the box is 54 cm, what is the volume of the box?

   A. 852 cm^3

   B. 970 cm^3

   C. 4,546 cm^3

   D. 5,832 cm^3

9) What is the slope of a line that is parallel to the line $8x - 2y = 18$?

   A. -4

   B. 4

   C. 6

   D. 18

10) Which of the following graphs represents the compound inequality $-12 \leq$

$3x - 15 < 3$?

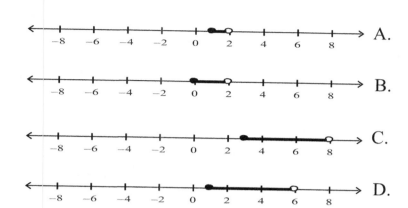

11) What is the value of the expression $3(x - 2y) + (2 - x)^2$ when $x = -2$ and

$y = 3$?

A. -8

B. 10

C. 16

D. 12

12) Two dice are thrown simultaneously, what is the probability of getting a sum

of 7 or 9?

A. $\dfrac{1}{18}$

B. $\dfrac{1}{9}$

C. $\dfrac{3}{10}$

D. $\dfrac{5}{18}$

13) A bank is offering 1.5% simple interest on a savings account. If you deposit $8,500 how much interest will you earn in two years?

    A. $200

    B. $255

    C. $1,110

    D. $5,200

14) What is the volume of a box with the following dimensions?

    Height = 3 cm   Width = 4 cm   Length = 8 cm

    A. $70\ cm^3$

    B. $40\ cm^3$

    C. $96\ cm^3$

    D. $100 cm^3$

15) A shirt costing $250 is discounted 20%. After a month, the shirt is discounted another 20%. Which of the following expressions can be used to find the selling price of the shirt?

    A. (250) (0.80)

    B. (250) − 250 (0.20)

    C. (250) (0.20) − (250) (0.20)

    D. (250) (0.8) (0.8)

16) Which graph corresponds to the following inequalities?

$$y \leq x + 3$$

$$2x + 3y \geq -6$$

A.

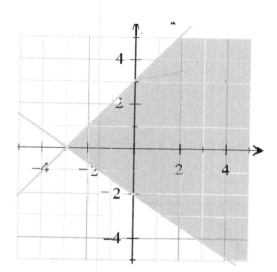

B.

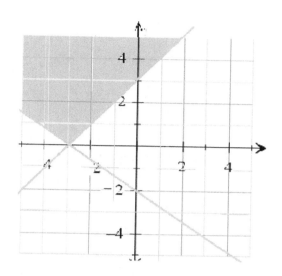

C.

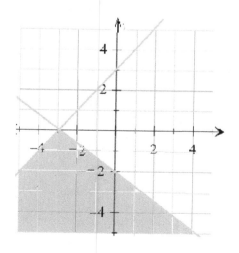

D.

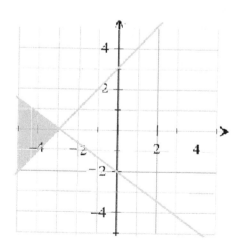

17) Mr. Carlos family are choosing a menu for their reception. They have 5 choices of appetizers, 9 choices of entrees, 7 choices of cake. How many different menu combinations are possible for them to choose?

    A. 120

    B. 300

    C. 315

    D. 450

18) What is the area of the shaded region?

    A. $86 \, ft^2$

    B. $120 \, ft^2$

    C. $184 \, ft^2$

    D. $304 \, ft^2$

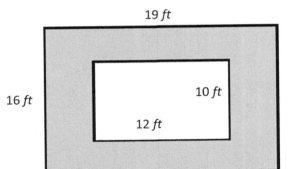

19) When a number is subtracted from 60 and the difference is divided by that number, the result is 4. What is the value of the number?

    A. 3

    B. 15

    C. 9

    D. 12

20) In two successive years, the population of a town is increased by 15% and 20%.

What percent of its population is increased after two years?

A. 25

B. 38

C. 20.5

D. 27

Practice Test 1

This is the End of this Section.

The Pennsylvania System of School Assessment

Practice Test 2

Mathematics

GRADE 7

❖ **20 Questions**

❖ **Calculators are permitted for this practice test**

Pennsylvania Department of Education Bureau of Curriculum, Assessment and Instruction— *Month Year*

1) If $x = -4$, which equation is true?

   A. $x(5x + 2) = -56$

   B. $7(3 - x) = 49$

   C. $4(2x + 9) = 19$

   D. $5x - 2 = -12$

2) In a bag of small balls $\frac{1}{3}$ are black, $\frac{1}{6}$ are white, $\frac{1}{12}$ are red and the remaining 15 blue. How many balls are white?

   A. 12

   B. 10

   C. 6

   D. 20

3) A boat sails 18 miles south and then 24 miles east. How far is the boat from its start point?

   A. 18

   B. 24

   C. 30

   D. 38

4) Simplify $3y^3(7x^2y)^2 =$

   A. $21x^4y^6$

   B. $14x^5y^7$

   C. $147x^4y^5$

   D. $147x^6y^7$

5) Sophia purchased a sofa for $502.32 The sofa is regularly priced at $546 What was the percent discount Sophia received on the sofa?

A. 18%

B. 8%

C. 92%

D. 22%

6) The score of Elise was half as that of Mia and the score of Stella was twice that of Mia. If the score of Stella was 100, what is the score of Elise?

A. 50

B. 10

C. 25

D. 45

7) A bag contains 15 balls: two green, four black, three blue, one brown, three red and two white. If 14 balls are removed from the bag at random, what is the probability that a brown ball has been removed?

A. $\frac{1}{15}$

B. $\frac{1}{14}$

C. $\frac{13}{14}$

D. $\frac{14}{15}$

8) What is the area of the shaded region?

A. 4π cm^2

B. 36π cm^2

C. 20π cm^2

D. 16π cm^2

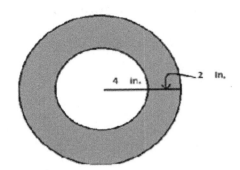

9) A pizza cut into 8 parts. Elise and her sister Etta ordered two pizzas. Elise ate $\frac{1}{4}$ of her pizza and Etta ate $\frac{3}{8}$ of her pizza. What part of the two pizzas was left?

A. $\frac{11}{16}$

B. $\frac{1}{16}$

C. $\frac{5}{16}$

D. $\frac{5}{12}$

10) The marked price of a computer is D dollar. Its price decreased by 50% in January and later increased by 30 % in February. What is the final price of the computer in D dollar?

A. 0.65 D

B. 0.68 D

C. 0.50 D

D. 1.30 D

11) $[6 \times (-20) + 18] - (12) + [7 \times 9] \div 3 =$?

Write your answer in the box below.

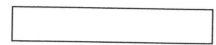

12) From last year, the price of gasoline has increased from $1.15 per gallon to $1.61 per gallon. The new price is what percent of the original price?

A. 35 %

B. 50 %

C. 140 %

D. 150 %

13) What is the median of these numbers? 8, 36, 20, 29, 86, 49, 47

A. 20

B. 36

C. 49

D. 47

14) The following trapezoid are similar. What is the value of x ?

A. 7

B. 10

C. 18

D. 22

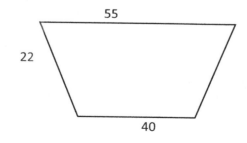
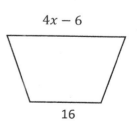

15) Three times the price of a laptop is equal to six times the price of a computer.

    If the price of laptop is $400 more than the computer, what is the price of the

    computer?

    A. 450

    B. 200

    C. 700

    D. 400

16) What is the volume of the following square pyramid?

    A. 647 m^3

    B. 984 m^3

    C. 1,728 m^3

    D. 2,480 m^3

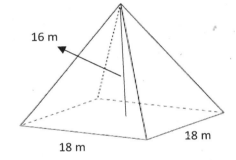

17) A bank is offering 1.5% simple interest on a savings account. If you deposit

    $13,000 how much interest will you earn in four years?

    A. $780

    B. $680

    C. $1,300

    D. $2,600

18) Which of the following points lies on the line $5x + 2y = -11$?

    A. $(2, 3)$

    B. $(-3, 2)$

    C. $(-3, 4)$

    D. $(2, 0)$

19) An angle is equal to one fifth of its supplement. What is the measure of that angle?

    A. 30

    B. 40

    C. 45

    D. 90

20) John traveled 160 km in 4 hours and Alice traveled 250 km in 5 hours. What is the ratio of the average speed of John to average speed of Alice?

    A. $3: 5$

    B. $4: 3$

    C. $4: 5$

    D. $5: 4$

Practice Test 2

This is the End of this Section.

Answers and Explanations

PSSA Practice Tests

Answer Key

✻ Now, it's time to review your results to see where you went wrong and what areas you need to improve!

PSSA - Mathematics

Practice Test - 1				Practice Test - 2			
1	C	11	A	1	B	11	−93
2	B	12	D	2	C	12	C
3	D	13	B	3	C	13	B
4	D	14	C	4	C	14	A
5	D	15	D	5	B	15	D
6	C	16	A	6	C	16	C
7	C	17	C	7	D	17	A
8	D	18	C	8	C	18	B
9	B	19	D	9	A	19	A
10	D	20	B	10	D	20	C

Practice Test 1
PSSA - Mathematics
Answers and Explanations

1) Answer: C

Use this formula: Percent of Change

$$\frac{\text{New Value} - \text{Old Value}}{\text{Old Value}} \times 100\,\%$$

$$\frac{6,000 - 10,000}{10,000} \times 100\,\% = 40\,\% \quad \text{and} \quad \frac{3,600 - 6,000}{6,000} \times 100\,\% = 40\,\%$$

2) Answer: B

$$\frac{3}{7}x + \frac{1}{6} = \frac{1}{3} \Rightarrow \frac{3}{7}x = \frac{1}{6} \Rightarrow x = \frac{7}{3} \times \frac{1}{6} \Rightarrow x = \frac{7}{18}$$

3) Answer: D

Surface Area of a cylinder $= 2\pi r\,(r + h)$,

The radius of the cylinder is 4 ($8 \div 2$) inches and its height is 12 inches. Therefore,

Surface Area of a cylinder $= 2\pi\,(4)\,(4 + 12) = 128\,\pi$

4) Answer: D

$$\text{Probability} = \frac{\text{number of desired outcomes}}{\text{number of total outcomes}} = \frac{15}{11 + 15 + 12 + 12} = \frac{15}{50} = \frac{3}{10}$$

5) Answer: D

Change the numbers to decimal and then compare.

$$\frac{3}{5} = 0.6; \quad 0.65; \quad 97\% = 0.97; \quad \frac{11}{9} = 1.2 \quad \text{Therefore,} \quad \frac{11}{9} > 97\% > 0.65 > \frac{3}{5}$$

6) Answer: C

Input $(-1, 5)$ in the $8x + 4y = 12$ formula instead of x and y. So, we have:

$8(-1) + 4(5) = 12 \Rightarrow -8 + 20 = 12$

7) Answer: C

$$\text{average (mean)} = \frac{\text{sum of terms}}{\text{number of terms}} \Rightarrow 70 = \frac{\text{sum of terms}}{35} \Rightarrow \text{sum} = 70 \times 35 = 2,450$$

The difference of 87 and 78 is 9. Therefore, 9 should be subtracted from the sum.

$2,450 - 9 = 2,441$

$$\text{mean} = \frac{\text{sum of terms}}{\text{number of terms}} \Rightarrow \text{mean} = \frac{2,441}{35} = 69.74$$

8) Answer: D

If the length of the box is 54, then the width of the box is one third of it, 18, and the height of the box is 6 (one third of the width). The volume of the box is:

$$V = l \times w \times h = (54) \times (18) \times (6) = 5,832$$

9) Answer: B

The equation of a line in slope intercept form is: $y = mx + b$

Solve for y.

$$8x - 2y = 18 \Rightarrow -2y = 18 - 8x \Rightarrow y = (18 - 8x) \div (-2) \Rightarrow y = 4x - 9$$

The slope of this line is 4. Parallel lines have same slopes.

10) Answer: D

Solve for x.

$$-12 \le 3x - 15 < 3 \Rightarrow \text{(add 15 all sides)}$$

$$-12 + 15 \le 3x - 15 + 15 < 3 + 15 \Rightarrow 3 \le 3x < 18$$

$$\Rightarrow \text{(divide all sides by 3) } 1 \le x < 6$$

x is between 1 and 6. Choice D represent this inequality.

11) Answer: A

When $x = -2$ and $y = 3$,

Substitute: $3(x - 2y) + (2 - x)^2 = 3\big((-2) - 2(3)\big) + \big(2 - (-2)\big)^2$

$$= 3(-2 - 6) + (2 + 2)^2 = -24 + 16 = -8$$

12) Answer: D

The options to get sum of 7: (1 & 6), (6 & 1), (2 & 5), (5 & 2), (4 & 3), (3 & 4), so we have 6 options

The options to get sum of 9: (4 & 5), (5 & 4), (3 & 6), (6 & 3), we have 4 options.

To get the sum of 4 or 9 for two dice, we have 10 options: $6 + 4 = 10$

Since, we have $6 \times 6 = 36$ total options, the probability of getting a sum of 7 and 9 is

10 out of 36 or $\dfrac{10}{36} = \dfrac{5}{18}$

13) Answer: B

Use simple interest formula:

$I = prt$ (I = interest, p = principal, r = rate, t = time)

$I = (8,500)(0.015)(2) = 255$

14) Answer: C

Volume of a box = length × width × height = 8 × 4 × 3 = 96

15) Answer: D

To find the discount, multiply the number by (100% − rate of discount).

Therefore, for the first discount we get: (250) (100% − 20%) = (250) (0.8)

For the next 20 % discount: (250) (0.8) (0.8)

16) Answer: A

For each option, choose a point in the solution part and check it on both inequalities.

$$y \leq x + 3$$

$$2x + 3y \leq -6$$

A. Point (−1, 1) is in the solution section. Let's check the point in both inequalities.

$1 \leq -1 + 3$, It works

$2(-1) + 3(1) \geq -6 \Rightarrow 1 \geq -6$, it works (this point works in both)

B. Let's choose this point (−3, 3); $3 \leq -3 + 3$, That's not true!

C. Let's choose this point (−2, −5); $-5 \leq -2 + 3$, It works

$2(-2) + 3(-5) \geq -6 \Rightarrow -19 \geq -6$, That's not true!

D. Let's choose this point (−5, 0); $0 \leq -5 + 3$, That's not true!

17) Answer: C

To find the number of possible outfit combinations, multiply number of options for each factor: 5 × 9 × 7 = 315

18) Answer: C

Use the area of rectangle formula ($s = a \times b$).

To find area of the shaded region subtract the smaller rectangle from bigger rectangle.

$S_1 - S_2 = (19ft \times 16t) - (12ft \times 10ft) \Rightarrow S_1 - S_2 = 304ft^2 - 120ft^2 = 184ft^2$

19) Answer: D

Let the number be x. Then:

$\frac{60-x}{x}=4 \rightarrow 4x=60-x \rightarrow 5x=60 \rightarrow x=12$

20) Answer: B

The population is increased by 15% and 20%. 15% increase changes the population to 115% of original population.

For the second increase, multiply the result by 120%.

$(1.15)\times(1.20)=1.38=138\%$

38 percent of the population is increased after two years.

Practice Test 2

PSSA - Mathematics

Answers and Explanations

1) Answer: B

Only option B is correct. Other options don't work in the equation.

$7(3 - (-4)) = 49$

2) Answer: C

Let x be the number of balls. Then:

$\frac{1}{3}x + \frac{1}{6}x + \frac{1}{12}x + 15 = x$

$(\frac{1}{3} + \frac{1}{6} + \frac{1}{12})x + 15 = x$

$(\frac{7}{12})x + 15 = x \Rightarrow x = 36$

In the bag of small balls $\frac{1}{6}$ are white, then: $\frac{36}{6} = 6$

There are 6 white balls in the bag.

3) Answer: C

Use the information provided in the question to draw the shape.

Use Pythagorean Theorem: $a^2 + b^2 = c^2$

$18^2 + 24^2 = c^2 \Rightarrow 324 + 576 = c^2 \Rightarrow 900 = c^2 \Rightarrow c = 30$

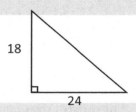

4) Answer: C

Simplify: $3y^3(7x^2y)^2 = 3y^3(49x^4y^2) = 147x^4y^5$

5) Answer: B

The question is this: 502.32 is what percent of 546?

Use percent formula: part $= \frac{\text{percent}}{100} \times$ whole

$502.32 = \frac{\text{percent}}{100} \times 546 \Rightarrow 502.32 = \frac{\text{percent} \times 726}{100} \Rightarrow 50{,}232 = \text{percent} \times 546 \Rightarrow \text{percent} = \frac{50{,}232}{546} = 92$

502.32 is 92 % of 546. Therefore, the discount is: 100% – 92% = 8%

6) Answer: C

If the score of Stella was 100, then the score of Mia is 50. Since, the score of Elise was half as that of Mia, therefore, the score of Elise is 25.

7) Answer: D

If 14 balls are removed from the bag at random, there will be one balls in the bag. The probability of choosing one brown ball is 1 out of 15. Therefore, the probability of not choosing one brown ball is 14 out of 15 and the probability of having not brown balls after removing 14 balls is the same.

8) Answer: C

To find the area of the shaded region, find the difference of the area of two circles. (S_1: the area of bigger circle. S_2: the area of the smaller circle)

Use the area of circle formula. $S = \pi r^2$

$S1 - S2 = \pi (4+2)^2 - \pi(4in)^2 \Rightarrow S1 - S2 = \pi 36in^2 - \pi 16\,in^2 \Rightarrow S1 - S2 = 20\pi\,in^2$

9) Answer: A

Elise ate $\frac{1}{4}$ of 8 parts of his pizza that it means 2 parts out of 8 parts ($\frac{1}{4}$ of 8 parts = $x \Rightarrow$ $x = 2$) and left 6 parts.

Etta ate $\frac{3}{8}$ of 8 parts of her pizza that it means 3 parts out of 8 parts ($\frac{3}{8}$ of 8 parts = $x \Rightarrow$ $x = 3$) and left 5 parts.

Therefore, they ate (3 + 2) parts out of (8+8) parts of their pizza and left (6 + 5) parts out of (8 + 8) parts of their pizza. It means: $\frac{11}{16}$

After simplification we have: $\frac{11}{16}$

10) Answer: A

To find the discount, multiply the number by (100% – rate of discount).

Therefore, for the first discount we get: (D) (100% – 50%) = (D) (0.50) = 0.50 D

For increase of 30 %: (0.50 D) (100% + 30%) = (0.50 D) (1.30) = 0.65 D = 65% of D

11) Answer: -93

Use PEMDAS (order of operation):

$[6 \times (-20) + 18] - (12) + [7 \times 9] \div 3 =$

$= [-120 + 18] - 12 + [63] \div 3 = [-102] - 12 + 21 = -93$

12) Answer: C

The question is this: 1.61 is what percent of 1.15?

Use percent formula: part $= \frac{\text{percent}}{100} \times$ whole

$= \frac{\text{percent}}{100} \times 1.15 \Rightarrow 1.61 = \frac{\text{percent} \times 1.15}{100} \Rightarrow 161 = \text{percent} \times 1.15$

$\Rightarrow \text{percent} = \frac{161}{1.15} = 140$

13) Answer: B

Write the numbers in order: 8, 20, 29, 36, 47, 49, 86

Since we have 7 numbers (7 is odd), then the median is the number in the middle,

which is 36.

14) Answer: A

Write the ratio and solve for x.

$\frac{55}{40} = \frac{4x-6}{16} \Rightarrow 40(4x - 6) = 55 \times 16 \Rightarrow 4x - 6 = 880 \div 40 \Rightarrow 4x - 6 = 22 \Rightarrow x = 7$

15) Answer: D

Let L be the price of laptop and C be the price of computer.

$3(L) = 6(C)$ and $L = \$400 + C$

Therefore, $3(\$400 + C) = 6C \Rightarrow \$1,200 + 3C = 6C \Rightarrow C = \$400$

16) Answer: C

Use the volume of square pyramid formula.

$V = \frac{1}{3} a^2 h \Rightarrow V = \frac{1}{3}(18m)^2 \times 16m \Rightarrow V = 1,728m^3$

17) Answer: A

Use simple interest formula:

$I = prt$ (I = interest, p = principal, r = rate, t = time)

$I = (13,000)(0.015)(4) = 780$

18) Answer: B

Input the points instead of x and y in the formula. Only option B works in the equation.

$5x + 2y = -11$

$5(-3) + 2(2) = -11$

19) Answer: A

The sum of supplement angles is 180. Let x be that angle. Therefore,

$x + 5x = 180$

$6x = 180$, divide both sides by 6: $x = 30$

20) Answer: C

The average speed of John is: $160 \div 4 = 40$ km

The average speed of Alice is: $250 \div 5 = 50$ km

Write the ratio and simplify: $40: 50 \Rightarrow 4: 5$

"End"

Made in the USA
Middletown, DE
16 April 2021